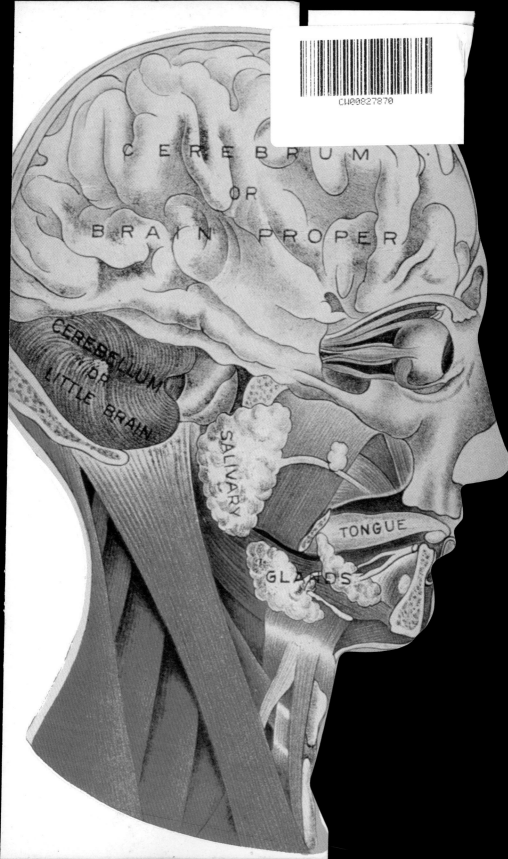

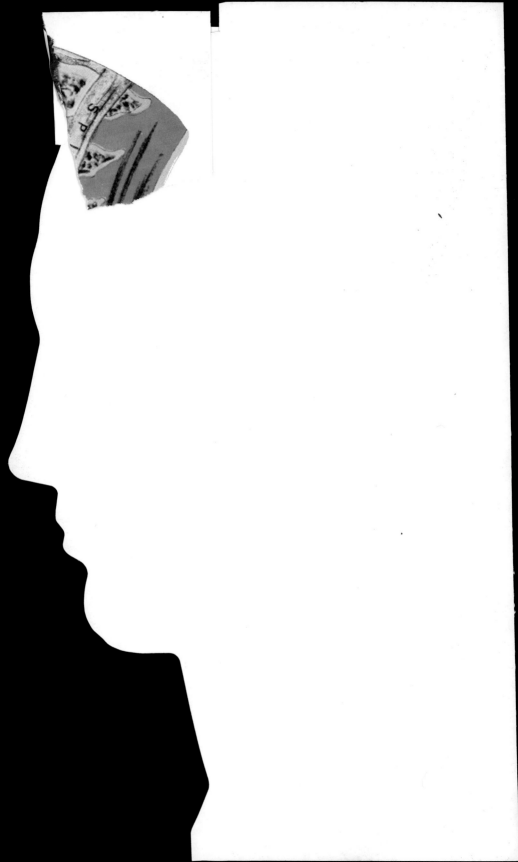

INDEX.

VITALOGY

AN

ENCYCLOPEDIA OF HEALTH AND HOME

ADAPTED for the HOME, the LAYMAN, the FAMILY

E. H. RUDDOCK, M. D.,

Author of "A Text Book of Modern Medicine and Surgery"; "Consumption and Diseases of
the Lungs", "Essentials of Diet"; "The Vade Mecum"; "The Ladies' Manual";
"The Pocket Manual"; "The Stepping Stone"; "Diseases of
Infants and Children"; Etc.

Four Books Bound in One Volume

DEPARTMENTAL EDITORS

HYDROPATHY (WATER CURE)
Bathing, Etc.
J. D. CRAIG, M. D.

HOME TRAINING EXERCISE,
HYGIENE, SECRET OF LONGEVITY
C. D. M. CAMPBELL
DR. WM. KINNEAR

MENTAL THERAPEUTICS
MAGNETISM,
PALMISTRY, MIND CURE
DR. L. F. JORDAN
W. L. FLEMING, M. D.

PSYCHOLOGY, MORAL AND SEX
HYGIENE, MARRIAGE, CHILD
CULTURE
PROF. L. H. STANDISH
J. G. HOLLAND

Illustrated with Manikins, (Natural Colors) and Half-Tone Plates

1994

Published by APPLEWOOD BOOKS
18 North Road, Bedford, Massachusetts

Vitalogy was originally published in 1899. This edition has been reproduced from a copy of the 1930 edition, published by the Vitalogy Association of Chicago, which is now housed in the collection of the Palmer College Library, Palmer College of Chiropractics, Davenport, Iowa.

The Publisher would like to thank Colleen Combs of Curtis Management, Larry Rungren and Dianne Ryan of the Bedford Public Library, and Dennis Peterson and Glenda Wiese, of the Palmer College of Chiropractics.

ISBN: 1-55709-404-7

Thank you for purchasing an Applewood Book.
Applewood reprints America's lively classics – books from the past that are still of interest to modern readers. For a free copy of our current catalog, please write to Applewood Books, 18 North Road, Bedford, MA 01730.

10 9 8 7 6 5 4 3

WHAT TO READ FIRST IN THIS BOOK

TABLE *of* CONTENTS

ILLUSTRATIONS

DIVISION ONE.

FAMILY BED ROOM.

Who should and who should not occupy the same bed. Both health and life involved in this matter.

TO AVOID EXCESSIVE INDULGENCES.

Married persons should adopt more generally the rule of sleeping in separate rooms, or at least in separate beds, as is the almost universal custom in Germany and Holland. This rule being adopted, several very important advantages would result in regard to health and comfort.

Opportunity makes importunity. For example, if pastries are where they continually attract the attention of children, there is a want and a request for them; but if out of sight they would only be thought of when natural hunger came. So, if married persons slept in different rooms the indulgences would only be specially thought of when there existed a natural, healthy appetite for the same, and as food is the more enjoyable from the longer interval of fasting; so here. In this way troublesome temptations are escaped and a rational temperance would be practiced without inconvenience.

And it is well known, too, that if two persons, one sickly and the other healthy, occupy the same bed, one will become diseased without the sickly one becoming benefited. This is especially true when children sleep with old and feeble persons. Hence, it is seldom the case that both the wife and husband are in perfect health, in all respects, at all times; at least one party would be saved from injury by sleeping alone.

When two People may Sleep Together Advantageously.— Two people may often occupy the same bed to the decided benefit of both. For instance, when one is by nature full of positive electricity or magnetism, while the other's body is negative. In this case there is an insensible and gradual interchange of vital currents. The excess of positive goes out to the negative body, and it in turn gives of its over supply of negative to the positive body, and thus a normal and healthful condition is brought about. This must be the explanation of the numerous instances where a weak and semi-invalid woman marries a man not considered unusually strong and both become healthier and able to endure far more than either could before marriage. Each gives to the other without losing any essential part of themselves.

HOW CHILDREN ARE BORN EITHER BRIGHT OR STUPID.

Nearly all writers admit the power of ante-natal impressions. The effects, upon offspring, of the mother's fright during pregnancy are well known, and they are often supposed to result in the permanent deformity or idiocy of the child. These effects are frequently seen in what are called birth-marks. Equally potent, and frequently to the more observing equally patent, are the effects of loving and loathing, and the continued presence of sights hateful or agreeable to the mother. Upon these and like observations has been built what may now be called the Science of Ante-natal Education or Training. *There no longer remains any doubt that children may be born strong or weak, beautiful or ugly, talented or imbecile, good or bad, according to the will and wisdom of their parents. What would not a parent give to have his child mentally bright and physically handsome? Why, it could not be estimated in dollars and cents!*

This article should be read and studied by every parent, as none can afford to be without the information imparted here.

We should give to this the highest and most important act of our lives, whose consequences may extend to future generativns, a corresponding degree of care and painstaking. For this purpose, we should be in the highest and strongest physical health and vigor of which we are capable; and to secure this state, we should take that amount and quality of bodily exercise which are best calculated to produce it. At the same time, our mental faculties should be in their highest and most active condition. Then, the sentiment and passion of mutual love and attraction should be at their strongest, and the hour selected should be that time of the day when our whole nature is in its fullest force and highest vigor; this is not at night, when we are exhausted by fatigue, nor on waking in the morning, before our faculties are fully aroused.

Subsequent to conception, and before the birth of the child, much may be done by the mother for its future character and development. During the first four or five months of pregnancy, while nature is laying its foundation and framework, so to speak, of the future man or woman, the mother may contribute not a little to the strength and hardihoood of her child's constitution, by the faithful practice of a suitable system of exercise and regimen. Later, in the sixth and seventh months, when the brain is being formed and matured, she may stamp it with the very quality of her own tastes and pursuits. Surrounding herself with beautiful and cheerful objects, communing much with the best books and the most gifted minds, hearing the most eloquent speakers and living in the worlds of literature and art, she may give birth to a genius who will astonish the world and delight her own heart; or, reversing all this and giving her attention to the mean and the sordid, the effect will be seen in the lower and more incapable mental qualities of her offspring. As she sows in this season, so will she reap in the harvest-time of maternity.

Finally, the temper and character of her child will depend very greatly upon her own, especially during the last months of her pregnancy. Here and now she becomes almost omnipotent. Patient, serene, content, gentle, pure, unselfish, cheerful and happy, the sunny being that will be born of her will brighten and gladden all her life; while, if fretful, turbulent, discontented and unhappy during this period—and much more if she be positively vicious— she need not be surprised if she give birth to a public and private pest, that will break her own heart and be a curse to society. Nothing is now more certainly known, or better understood, among those who have given attention to this matter, than this potential effect of the moods of the mother upon the character of her child. If then she would see her children strong and healthy, graceful and beautiful, quick, sprightly, intelligent and gifted, cheerful, obedient and happy, virtuous and respected, the ornaments of society and the lights and jewels of her own heart and home, let her give heed to those immediate laws of ante-natal influence, some hint of which may be found in what we have said above.

JAMES RUSSELL LOWELL, M. D.

PARENTS CAN HAVE THEIR CHILDREN BORN WITH NOBLE GIFTS

On this subject Dr. Lowell wrote: *"Previous to the conceptional period more can be done for the coming child than can afterwards be done in years of school or college."*

This is the time to endow the coming child with intellectual capabilities—imparting to it either brilliancy, mediocrity or stupidity.

The law that brought into being, from among the common ranks of life, such men as Benjamin Franklin, Lincoln, Bismarck, Gladstone, Napoleon and hundreds of other gifted individuals, will do the same for all who comply with the simple, natural law.

Nature never works by chance. "The God of nature works through eternal law."

4

L. P. ELDREDGE'S SECOND CHILD

It has been fully tested and proven that children may be born talented or imbecile, with cheerful dispositions or gloomy ones, with kindly natures or harsh and sour ones, according to the will and wisdom of their parents.

L. P. ELDREDGE'S FIRST CHILD

L. P. Eldredge of Brooklyn, N. Y., states: "Neither my wife nor myself, previous to the conceptional period, nor during the next nine months, the period when the future child is fashioned or moulded with its mental faculties and other endowments, gave any attention to the effects that would be produced on it. But in the case of our second child, we did, and the result was a bright and intellectual child."

GIFTED MEN

Parents who desire their children endowed with abilities such as the noted men illustrated on the following pages, need only inform themselves and act accordingly. Grandparents, too, may be blessed with strong, healthy, brilliant grandchildren, if they will place in the hands of their sons and daughters the means of information.

More can be done at the period of time here indicated than can be done afterwards in years at college.

Born in a log cabin, he became the most famous leader of
his time.

The "Grand Old Man" Was a Merchant's Son.

Born in Obscurity, He Became a Renowned Commander

HEALTHFUL RESIDENCE

SUNLIGHT.

The importance of sunlight for physical development and preservation is not duly appreciated. Women and children, as well as men, in order to be healthy and well-developed, should spend a portion of each day where the sun can reach them directly, this being particularly necessary when there is a tendency to scrofula. Just as sprouts of potatoes in a dark cellar seek the light and are colorless until they come under its influence, and as vegetation goes on but imperfectly in places where sunlight does not freely enter, so children and adults who live almost entirely in dark kitchens, dingy alleys and badly lighted workshops are pale-cheeked and feeble. And it should be said that houses are only fit to be occupied at night that have been purified by the sun during the day. It has been pointed out by Dr. Ellis that women and children in huts and log-cabins which contain only one or two rooms remain healthy and strong; but that after the settler has built a house and furnished it with blinds and curtains, the women and children become pale-faced, bloodless, nervous and sickly; the daughters begin to die from consumption and the wives from the same, or from some other diseases peculiar to women. At the same time the adult males who live chiefly out of doors continue healthy.

The value of sunlight for animal development may be illustrated by such facts as the following: In decaying organic solutions, animalcules do not appear if light is excluded, but are readily organized when it is admitted. The tadpole kept in the dark does not pass on to development as a frog, but lives and dies a tadpole and is incapable of propagating his species. In the deep and narrow valleys among the Alps, where the direct rays of the sun are but little felt, cretinism, or a state of idiocy, more or less complete, commonly accompanied by an enormous goiter, prevails and is often hereditary.

How to Prepare a Room for Sun Baths. The simplest ar-
rangement for sun bathing is to choose the smallest and most quiet
room in the house which has two or more high windows. The lower
part of the windows may be protected by sash curtains or the glass rendered opaque, so no one can see in from the outside, by rubbing it
freely with soap, or covering it with whitewash. It is better, but not
necessary, to replace the window panes with ground glass or blue glass,
if these can be obtained readily. At the opposite side of the room from
the windows should be placed one or more of the largest mirrors or
reflectors available, so arranged as to reflect the light toward the chair
where it is proposed to sit during the bath, care being taken that the
sun's bright rays do not fall directly upon the mirror. The chair may
be a cane or rattan or any other open-work chair that will offer the
least interference to the sun light striking the body. A weak, sick or
crippled person might better recline in a hammock of some light open
net-work. The room of course must be well warmed in cool or cold
weather. When about to take the sun bath all clothing must be removed and the nude body presented to the sun's rays. It is, of course,
necessary to continue long enough in any one position to permit the
light to penetrate, which it will do in from five to fifteen minutes. The
bath itself may be prolonged from a brief ten or fifteen minutes to an
hour, or several hours, according to the person and conditions.

If the effect is in any way disagreeable the duration of the bath must
be shortened. It may be taken any time of the day most convenient
while the sun shines into the room prepared for the purpose. If one
suffers from any chronic complaint he should take the bath daily, taking care to have longer exposures in cloudy than in fair weather. The
actinic rays of the sun can reach the body when clouds interfere just
as they reach the photographer's sensitized plate and enable him to
take a picture on a cloudy day, but it takes a little longer. The actinic
rays, and most of the light rays, pass right through the clouds. It
must be remembered that in taking a photograph the picture is made
by the power of the actinic rays of the sun to decompose chemicals.
You cannot take a picture without the use of chemicals. Our bodies
are full of chemicals, oftentimes of such as are injurious and clog the
system. Some of these are decomposed by the sun in the sun bath and
are thus rendered harmless, or changed so that the system can throw
them off naturally and easily.

To make the sun bath most effective it is desirable to have the re-
flecting mirrors on two sides or three sides of the person, providing
they can be had, and it is better to have them covered with blue glass,
because blue glass lets through more readily than other glass the actinic rays and intercepts the others. But the blue glass is not absolutely necessary. It is an advantage to have all the windows which
admit sunlight into this room provided with blue glass, but this is not
essential. The essential thing is to have the sunlight and plenty of it
strike the skin on all parts of the body and especially over the region
of the vital organs.

How to Take a Sun Bath. Before entering a room in which

the sun bath is to be taken, the entire surface of the body should be sponged off with warm water (as warm as can conveniently be borne without discomfort), in which a few handfuls of salt have been dissolved, and immediately after sponging wipe thoroughly dry. Then, sitting upon a plain wooden or leather covered stool, or reclining in an open net-work hammock, the nude body should be exposed to the action of the sun, taking care that every portion of the body receives the sun's direct rays undisturbed for at least ten minutes at a time. If there is serious discomfort at first, it may be avoided by anointing the body after the sponging, with olive oil or a little vaseline. The exposure, if not agreeable, may at first be for a shorter period, gradually extending it to as long a time as circumstances will permit.

Transmits Ultra-Violet Rays—From highest authority it has been learned from a scientific standpoint that a real glass which transmits the ultra-violet rays has recently been invented by an English scientist, called Vitaglass. This glass contains a high proportion of quartz and certain ingredients not present in ordinary glass and transmits to the further limits of the sun's spectrum, the beneficial ultra-violet rays to which ordinary glass is not transparent.

Ordinary window glass permits the passage of some ultra-violet rays, but is quite opaque to rays of 3,100 or shorter wave length. However much sunlight may pour through ordinary glass into our rooms, it is entirely robbed of the vital rays. This new glass transmits light to the furthest rays of the sun's spectrum; i.e., 2,900 Angstroem units.

It is generally recognized today that the ideal recuperative treatment (especially in children's hospitals and in those dealing with tuberculosis complaints and rickets) consists in allowing the whole body to be bathed in the natural ultra-violet rays of sunshine. This may be carried out in comfort and convenience in rooms and special sun parlors having roofs or windows glazed with Vitaglass, as this new glass is termed.

Not Expensive—Its cost is not a great deal more than ordinary glass. In a 72-bed children's hospital in New York State, for example, the extra cost for this glass in the east, south and west sides of the building amounted to about $1,100. It has been specified for several other important hospitals in the East.

In England, not only is it being used for hospitals and private houses, but some very good results have been attained by its use in the improvement of the health of tropical animals—lions, tigers and monkeys—confined in their winter quarters in the London Zoo.

In view of the tremendous amount of attention now being paid to heliotherapy in this and other countries today, and its increasing use in many different diseases and conditions, this new glass has great possibilities of usefulness.

As a Protection from Disease—During the prevalence of certain epidemic diseases the inhabitants who occupy houses on the side of the street upon which the sun shines directly are less subject to the disorder than those who live on the shaded side. In all cities visited by the cholera the greatest number of deaths come in narrow streets, and on the sides of those having a northern exposure, where the salutary beams of the sun are excluded.

Except in severe inflammatory diseases of the eyes or brain the very common practice of darkening the sick-room is a very imprudent one. The restorative influence of daylight is thus excluded, and also the grateful and natural succession of light and darkness which favors sleep at the appropriate time and divests the period of sickness of the monotony and weariness of perpetual night.

Essential to Physical Development—Sunlight is important in the development and preservation of the physical system. In confirmation of this statement we have only to refer to the fact that children who are kept in dark alleys, cellars, factories and mines are frequently afflicted with rickets and various deformities and swelling of the bones, and especially with troubles of the spine. This occurs not only among the poor, who live in dark, damp places, but among the rich, who live in fine, dry, airy dwelllings, but keep their children a considerable portion of the time in-doors, secluded from the sun's light and deprived of exercise. As vegetables lose their healthy color and strength when deprived of sunlight, so with children: Their muscles become soft and delicate, the nervous system deranged, the digestive organs enfeebled, the blood watery and pale, and the skin loses its healthy, ruddy complexion and has a pale, sickly hue. People who live in houses much shaded by trees are more subject to certain forms of disease than those whose dwellings are freely exposed to the sun. Shade-trees should be at a distance from the house, that they may afford a grateful retreat for the hot days, and never so near the house as to shade the buildings or the windows. A model situation, in respect to external ventilation and sunlight, is exemplified in the illustration on page 56.

Admit Sunlight to Rooms—When the ladies of this country take as deep an interest in their own healthful development and the well-being of their children, as they now do in the elegant gloom of their parlors, and will give free admittance to the life-giving light of the sun during the entire day, regardless of the fact that it may dim the bright colors of the carpets and hangings, thinking more of dissipating dampness, mould and the effluvia of human bodies—those fruitful causes of disease—than of preserving by darkness the seeming freshness of their furniture and apartments, we shall have fewer unhappy families, fewer mothers will wear their lives out in the servile care of puny and sickly children, and fewer husbands will find their severest toil in the nursing cares of their home and be obliged to return to their business or labor in the morning more wearied than they left it the previous evening;

SUN BATH

New methods of using sunbeams for curing disease.

Restores the feeble and invigorates the debilitated better than any drug remedy ever compounded by the druggist. The Ultra-violet rays admitted through quartz glass have wonderful healing qualities.

If nature has a panacea for human ills and a prevention of every human ill, a universal remedy—that potent draft is sunlight.

Right now we know that sunlight will cure as well as prevent rickets; will both cure and prevent tuberculosis in man and beast; will cure some cases of cancer; will heal old ulcers that other measures will not heal; will cure some skin conditions, and will favorably influence the thyroid gland.

It has the power to build up simple, chemical compounds into the red coloring matter of the blood; into the green coloring matter of plants and into the various ferments, vitamines and organic chemicals found in them.

The power to analyze or to change higher compounds into lower ones is common, but there are only a few agencies that can build simpler compounds into higher ones. That, light can do.

The length of the vibrations of light range from almost inconceivably short ones to the lengths that are used in the radio. The eye can only recognize a small part of this ray. The great bulk of it lies above and below what the eye can see. About those parts of the ray which can be seen we know much.

Rollier of Switzerland, who has written special articles on sunlight treatment for the British Journal of Tuberculosis, and who has treated people with this method in Leysen, Switzerland, for many years, says the best methods of treating acne, pimples, blackheads and facial blemishes is by the sunlight method. It should be easy to put this statement to the test. Along the beaches on any hot day there are thousands of people garbed in a way that makes observation of the skin easy.

Rollier says that sun pigmenting is a cure for all of the great group of skin diseases which result from poor nutrition of the integument. It is likewise good for poorly nourished muscles. It is much the best remedy for varicose ulcers, old sores and fistulous tracts. The forms of tuberculosis in which it is most helpful are scrofula, gland tuberculosis, skin tuberculosis, and bone tuberculosis. It should not be used in cases of lung tuberculosis that are in the fever stage. In other cases of lung tuberculosis, it must be used cautiously.

Treatment—The sunlight treatment is begun by exposure of the feet to the open sunshine for five minutes on the first day. The foot is selected because it is the part of the body farthest removed from the disease. One week from the first day of exposure, the schedule of treatment calls for:

Back, 5 minutes; chest 10 minutes; abdomen, 15 minutes; thighs, 20 minutes; legs, 25 minutes; feet, 30 minutes.

In summer time the treatments are given between 6 and 9 in the morning. In winter, they can be given any time.

The Ultraviolet rays sunshine when admitted through quartz crystal glass give more powerful healing qualities. Usual size of glass 5 by 7 inches.

IMPORTANCE OF PHYSICAL EDUCATION.

A proper development of the physical system should be ensured during childhood and early youth, for otherwise the opportunity is in a great measure lost forever, and a comparatively puny and delicate body and a life-time of suffering and disappointed hopes are almost inevitable. But if the intellect be neglected during the same time, while a healthy body is secured, the result is much less serious. An individual may not even know his letters at the age of sixteen or eighteen years, and yet with industry get a good practical education. The following important facts are lost sight of, or not known or attended to by many parents and educators, namely: If we strive prematurely to develop the intellect of a child by undue application, an unnatural flow of blood is directed to the brain to supply the great activity and consequent waste which are thus created in this organ; therefore, the rest of the body suffers, because an excessive amount of blood has been diverted from its legitimate uses. Nor is this all, for the premature development of a part of the system is necessarily but an imperfect development of even that part. For this reason we rarely hear of our precocious children in after life as distinguished men or women. It is a matter of no small surprise to many that such " smart children " do not attain a higher rank in after life.

Consequence of Neglect.—The secret lies in the fact before stated. No one disputes the very great importance of physical education for the young; yet we have but to look around us at the puny, pale-faced, deformed children to see how fearfully this important part of education is neglected. And this is not only the case with young children; the neglect extends to older ones; to the students in many of our higher institutions of learning, in which many of the teachers are very censurable for permitting their studious pupils to work too much, and to have too many studies at the same time, to the neglect of physical culture. We are glad that in some few of our cities and towns men are becoming awakened to the importance of this matter. A change is greatly needed in our system of education, from the common school up, for in its present condition it is productive of much disease, insanity and physical deformity.

Students Principal Sufferers.—It is melancholy, indeed, in our institutions of learning to see so many puny-looking young men and women: hollow chests, round shoulders and bending body are characteristics of our students, and premature old age and disease carry off but too many of our most gifted men and

women. In some of our female institutions of learning as high
as thirty-seven per cent. of those who had been attendants have
died within two years after leaving school. Students as a general
rule are inclined to become listless and indolent; therefore they
should be required, as a matter of duty, to spend several hours during the middle of the day in regular, active, systematic exercise
and physical training, with active amusements. A double advantage is thus derived; for being occupied a portion of the time during the day they will be compelled to spend their evenings at study,
instead of in dissipation and folly. No doubt our present system
of education is very imperfect, though the day of its radical amend-
ment may be distant. The force of example and training seems
all-powerful. Teachers are educated to teach, and cannot well help
teaching as they are taught. The orthodoxy of education is of the
most proscriptive sort. To differ, to innovate, to adapt instruction,
either in kind or degree, to the capacity and mental bent of the
pupil would be certainly a perilous experiment, even could a teacher
be found sufficiently bold and original to design and attempt such
a thing. No doubt he would be ostracised, both by the profession
and the patron. We want our children educated in the good old
way; their minds stretched upon the rack which cracked the mental
sinews of their fathers and mothers; their intellectual stature
adapted to the proportions of the old Procrustean bed; their education to result in mental uniformity. Of course we all see that this
is silly; that it would be quite as reasonable to design and seek to
compass for our children an equal measure of physical strength and
weight; that the higher mathematics, the dead languages and many
of the arts now attempted to be taught in the public schools are
totally impracticable—not to say useless—to the large majority of
the pupils; but we go on in the same old fashion. Every child must
be classed and graded and put through the same mechanical drill.
It is quite certain that many are stultified and some ruined by the
process. But that makes no difference, it is the fashion; it is the
accepted theory of our age and country that all children should be
educated, and educated in the same way. Of course both these
propositions are outrages upon common sense. The vast majority
must be "hewers of wood and drawers of water," laborers and
common servants; and their partial or complete education, even
were the latter practicable, which it is not, must defeat the ends of
civilization, and more or less disorganize society. Such has been
the effect hitherto; it is patent to the observation of all men; servants and laborers are growing scarcer, and idlers, vagabonds, tramps,
thieves and robbers being multiplied year by year. This is the
natural and necessary effect of the system of popular education;
the servant is made to feel himself as good as his master, and the
laborer quite the social equal of his employer. What wonder that
these scorn service and labor and prefer to live by their wits?

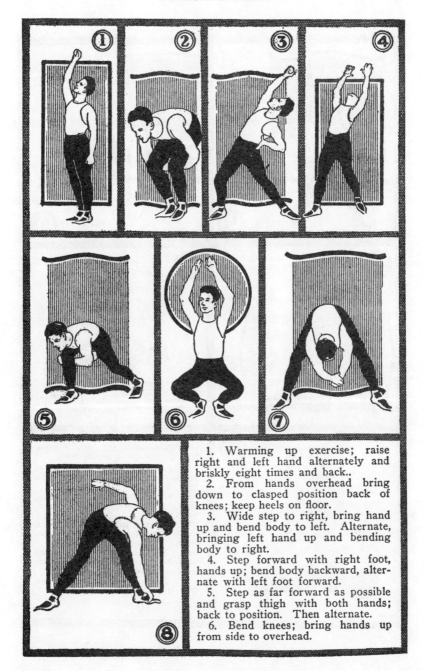

1. Warming up exercise; raise right and left hand alternately and briskly eight times and back..

2. From hands overhead bring down to clasped position back of knees; keep heels on floor.

3. Wide step to right, bring hand up and bend body to left. Alternate, bringing left hand up and bending body to right.

4. Step forward with right foot, hands up; bend body backward, alternate with left foot forward.

5. Step as far forward as possible and grasp thigh with both hands; back to position. Then alternate.

6. Bend knees; bring hands up from side to overhead.

7. Feet astride and arms extended, bring them to swing, as illustrated.

8. Feet apart; bring right hand to left foot. Alternate, left hand to right foot.

9. Feet astride, hands up; then hop, stride., hop, stride, bringing feet together on hop.

10. Sprinter's stride; hands on ground, hop from one foot to other, bringing alternate foot forward.

11. Flex knees to abdomen, pulling them in with hands. Alternate; then bring both knees up together.

12. Bring feet overhead, and then come to sitting position as in 13.

13. See 12.

Fig. 1. From Position bring hands up and outward in wide circle until backs of palms reach overhead, inhaling as you bring hands up; exhale as you bring them down. Do slowly five times.

Fig. 2. From Position bring hands to shoulders, fingers turned in; knuckles out; elbows close to body. Do five times.

Fig. 3. From Position bring hands up to almost straight line on chest, elbows in line with shoulders, wrists straight, palms down, fingers nearly together; fling arms out wide. Back. Do five times on sharp command.

Fig. 4. From Position extend arms full length; keep rest of body firm; begin to make circles with extended hands and arms; begin with small ones and increase to circles of as large dimensions as you can.

Fig. 5. Assume good standing position, bend trunk forward until it is at right angles to legs; exhale on downward move; back to position, inhaling.

Fig. 6. Arms over head, fingers clasped bend to right five times, then to left five times. Keep arms close to head, knees straight, and feet firmly on round.

Fig. 7. Knees straight, twist trunk to right, at same time extending arms sideward. Then to left, inhaling on twist, exhaling on return to Position.

Fig. 8. Raise arms overhead; bend trunk forward and swing arms downward between legs; raise trunk and bend backward, swinging arms up over head again.

Fig. 9. Assume correct standing position, feet apart, arms out at sides; twist waist to left and touch finger tips of right hand to toes of left foot. Reverse. When you can touch the toe try to touch the floor on level with the heel, for that involves greater waist twisting.

Fig. 10. Rise on toes. Bend knees and extend arms sideward, squat slowly, keeping body erect. Go down as far as you can; back. Repeat five times. Until you get a balance control you may place hands on hips and go down.

The best time to exercise is in the morning, upon rising and before an open window, in dress that is unrestricting. Take the exercise in groups—say four the first week and four more the second, the balance the third week. Don't begin on all ten. You will be a little stiff at first, but if you follow the exercises with a bath and a good rubbing, there will be little discomfort.

Squatting Exercises—The squatting exercise possesses more merit than almost any other single exercise known. If practiced five minutes daily, morning and night, it will keep you in excellent trim. Especially does this exercise strengthen the muscles of the spine and abdomen, and for reducing superfluous fat on hips and abdomen it is wonderfully effective. It also strengthens the ankles and increases the flexibility of the knee joints.

Stand erect with the feet nearly together and hands resting on your hips. Rise upon the toes, then sink the body to the floor in a squatting posture, bending the knees sharply until the thighs and legs are doubled upon each other and the weight of the entire body is supported by the toes. You must keep your trunk perfectly erect throughout the movement. Return to the original position and repeat twelve times to begin with, gradually increasing to twenty or thirty times.

To improve the upper part of your body this squatting exercise is done in the same way as described above with the addition of the use of the arms in the following manner: Instead of putting the hands on the hips, stand erect with the arms at the side of the body. Then swing your arms laterally and above your head or stretched sideward, at the same time inhaling deeply through the nostrils, and sink the body to the floor in a squatting posture. This is a wonderful exercise to expand the chest and develop the bust, arms and neck, and bring into play all the extensors of the back, giving grace, strength and better carriage to the body.

RULES OF HYGIENE

1. Get fresh air into your system by walking at least a mile or two a day. Keep your bedroom window wide open at night.
2. Sleep eight or nine hours.
3. Don't neglect your daily bath.
4. Drink at least six glasses of water a day.
5. Evacuate the bowels daily. Food, water, and exercises are the best regulators.
6. Chew your food slowly.
7. Choose your food wisely. Eat some coarse and hard foods like crusts, toasts, hard biscuits, hard fruits, fibrous vegetables every day for exercising the jaws and to improve the condition of the teeth. Eat plentifully of vegetables and fruits and bran breads. Eat regularly.
8. Have your teeth examined twice a year by a dentist. Brush them after every meal and before retiring.

GYMNASTIC EXERCISE.

There are many who do not appreciate the importance of such exercise, and its bearing on the development of the physical organization. To judge of its favorable effects it is only necessary to observe some of the results of such exercise—the vigor imparted and the muscular development produced. Every city and village should be furnished with a gymnasium; and all, both male and female, old and young, who have no other form of exercise, should regularly resort to it. Many good people imagine that there is no necessity for gymnastic exercises, because they are a novelty, a thing of to day, and never heard of in the times of our stout old fathers. Why, they think, should we forsake the customs of our ancestors in favor of this new-fangled theory of romps? Our children will do very well, if they are as strong and vigorous as their fathers and grandfathers; and *they* had none of these modern inventions to help them to grow into men of might and mould. But these honest souls do not reflect that times have changed, and that the people have changed with them. We have no longer the same people, the same customs, or the same country. Then we had no large cities, and sedentary occupations were almost unknown. The men were farmers, herdsmen and hunters. The women toiled at the wheel, the loom, in active domestic service, and not infrequently a-field with the men. Together they lived, for the most part, in the open country or in small villages. A common necessity turned their daily life into gymnastic exercise. They ate sparingly and slept soundly. They had no money to spend for French cooks and little time to waste in devising luxuries for their table. Factories, spinning-jennies and power-looms were unknown; labor-saving machines were not; life meant labor, for both man and woman. They were healthy then, almost as a matter of course. Their diet was simple, their drink pure and unstimulating, and their habits natural and hardy. If "there were giants in those days," as no doubt there were, they were hewed by the sharp chisel of circumstance out of the hardest granite of our nature. If their hardness would shame the degenerate men and women of our day, there was and is ample reason for all the difference, without credit to them or shame to us. They were simply the creatures of their time, as we are the creatures of our time.

Degenerative Influences of Luxury.—Now, both men and women have wealth, luxury and leisure almost without stint. There are large employments in the counting-room and at the desk.

The hardest workers are brain-workers. Moreover the mechanic, and even the farmer, is comparatively without exercise; he tends his machine or rides on his agricultural implement. The daily laborers, in the old, active sense of labor, are already in a minority, and that minority is growing smaller every day with the invention of new machinery and new applications of old machines. Our great cities shut up millions of people to lives of severest toil without any suitable or proper exercise. All the children of the wealthy, and many of those in moderate circumstances, are reared to do nothing useful, or to wait through life for the turning up of some lucky chance. The employments of the women consist of fancy-work, novel-reading and social dissipation. They have no health, no vigor, no stamina. They are utterly unfit to be wives and mothers. Late hours, luxurious living, bad air and want of exercise have made of them the mere effigies of women. Our young men, boys, and even some of our modern girls, who are distinguished or disgraced by the epithet "fast," are addicted to the use of tobacco and other poisonous stimulants. And against the encroachments of these insidious destroyers they can set up no defensive bulwarks of strong health and vigorous constitution. They, therefore, succumb and fall easy victims, where otherwise they might long resist and even overcome the enemy.

The Duty of Public Authorities.—All this may be remedied, in large part at least, by the establishing of public and free gymnasiums in every city and village of our land, or at least their universal association with educational institutions. It is the obvious duty of the State to provide for the physical welfare and development of her citizens, and this is her•true interest as well. To encourage her in this she has the good example of the best and strongest of the ancient states. The wisest governments of ancient and modern times have made this provision, for the plain reason that it was the great constituent and reservoir of their own strength. More than anything else it fosters virtue. There is something naturally antagonistic between vice and vigor. Idleness and luxury, on the other hand, are the natural parents of social evil; a whole brood of intemperate appetites and malignant passions are born of this couple.

No doubt the public-school system of our later years shows a wonderful advance in the direction of paternal government. The world has never seen anything like it. It goes before all thought and all theory. It outstrips the most radical speculation. It springs up like the product of magic in the silence and night of thought, and while the world's mind is asleep. And, once in being, its growth is as marvelous as was its birth. Already it fills the towns and villages of the land: its commissioners are almost sovereign legislators; it has become one of the great factors in political combinations; and it grows daily in practical and pecuniary importance. Very soon the rural districts must demand their fair proportion of modern educational privileges, and a few years hence we may see the palatial public school-house on every inhabited section of the country. What will come of all this we do not undertake to say. At all events the school system is a prodigy, at which the people of this country will do well to look long and carefully. We have only referred to it in passing, to demonstrate the propriety of that action of the government in establishing those institutions for physical culture and development, for which we plead. The argument is plain to any mind. If the State can do so much for the mental training of the children of the country, which is not always certain to make them better citizens, it can surely do something for the training of the body, which will certainly ensure for the rising generation, robust physical vigor and a higher intellectual stature.

METHODS OF OBTAINING EXERCISE.

Exercise strengthens and invigorates every function of the body, and is essential to health and long life. No one in health should neglect to walk a moderate distance every day, and if possible, in the country, where the pure and invigorating air can be freely inhaled. Walking is the healthiest as well as the most natural mode of exercise. Other things being equal, this will insure the proper action of every organ of the body. The walk for health should be diverisfied, and if possible include ascents and descents and varying scenery, and be alternated, when circumstances admit of it, with riding on horseback, active gardening or similar pursuits, and with gymnastics and games of various kinds. Calisthenics prevent deformities as well as cure them; a gymnasium should be attached to every school, whether for boys or girls. Athletic sports and manly exercise should form a part of the education of youth, nor should they be neglected in after life, especially by persons of sedentary pursuits. Many aches and pains would rapidly vanish if the circulation were quickened by a judicious and regular use of the muscles. These modes of exercise, practiced moderately and regularly, and varied from day to day, are much more advantageous than the exciting, immoderate and irregular exertions which characterize the ball-room, the hunting-field, and even the cricket-ground or the rowing-match, which are sometimes pursued so violently as to be followed by severe and permanent injury to the constitution. In the case of very feeble and infirm persons, carriage-exercise, if such it may be called, and frictions, by means of bath-sheets and gloves, over the surface of the body and extremities, are the best substitutes for active exertion.

Time for Exercise—The proper periods for exercise are when the system is not depressed by fasting or fatigue, nor oppressed by the process of digestion. The robust may take exercise before breakfast; but delicate persons, who often become faint from exercise at this time, and languid during the early part of the day, had better defer it till from one to three hours after breakfast. Exercise prevents disease by giving vigor and energy to the body and its various organs and members, and thus enables them to ward off or overcome the influence of the causes which tend to impair their integrity. It cures many diseases by equalizing the circulation and the distribution of nervous energy, thus invigorating and strengthening weak organs, and removing local torpor and congestion.

Invalids should always be moderate in their exercise; take only short walks, avoid fatigue and not stand in the open air. The best time for them is in the forenoon, arranged so that they can rest for half an hour before dinner. They should never take exercise immediately before a meal or going to bed.

Exercise for Ladies and Others—As exercise is essential to the preservation of health and development, the proper method of taking it is an important subject of inquiry. Very little, and in many instances no provision whatever has been made in our cities and towns in the way of proper play-grounds for children or adults, and therefore it becomes necessary to seek private methods of getting exercise. As people are deprived of an opportunity for athletic sports and games, a competent teacher of physical exercise has become almost a necessity; even more essential than is a teacher for some of the branches taught in our schools. There are many who are not aware of the different motions which the human body is capable of making, and require making to prevent diseases and deformity; hence the importance of such teachers. Nor is the necessity for such teachers confined to cities and villages, for the female portion of the population of our rural districts have, in a great degree, neglected out-door amusements and exercise until disease and deformity have become the prevalent result.

Outdoor Exercise for Girls—Ordinarily it is not fashionable for girls and ladies to engage in active, out-door sports, such as running, playing ball, rambling over fields, etc.; and if young girls do take part in them they are cruelly called romps and tomboys —as terms of reproach—as though girls have not as good a right to exercise, air, light, amusements, symmetry of form and consequent health and beauty, as boys. In the eyes of some it is not proper for young ladies to engage in any of the out-door employments which give vigor and health to young men. There are but few who would wish to see them engage in the hardest manual labor, side by side with men, but we should like to see every farm provided with a large garden and orchard, and to see ladies spend more of their time cultivating berries, fruits, flowers and vegetables in the open air, and less in useless fancy sewing. They would thus make their homes paradises, where wealth, beauty and happiness would abound, instead of places of discontent, deformity and disease. Let such a change be wrought and it would cause the young men of our country to seek happiness in the quiet and peace

of the domestic circle, surrounded by loving wives and happy children, instead of living bachelors, repelled by the fear of being yoked
to extravagant, lazy, sickly wives, and by visions of starving, sickly
and dying children.

The Exercise that Produces Health—But the exercise
which is taken to cure headache and its kindred evils may sometimes
cause that very thing. This happens when the exercise is not taken
regularly and a single opportunity is made too much of, and the
person unaccustomed to it practices it too long or too vigorously.
The fact is that out-door exercise gives the keenest physical enjoyment, and if, for instance, a young girl who has been closely shut
up in the house has a chance to take exercise in a pleasant way she
is very likely to go too far, and the troubles which follow the over-
exertion often cause the too careful mother to conclude that her
delicate child is not fit to be out doors at all, when in fact being
out regularly in good weather is the thing above all others she most
needs.

SLEEP AS A FACTOR IN HEALTH.

Very few people understand and still fewer appreciate the im·
portance of sound, regular, timely and refreshing sleep. Tissue-
waste, the consumption of the entire physical structure, from brain
to cuticle, goes on during all our waking hours. Sleep is the time
and the only time in which those reparative processes which may
overcome all this waste can take place. To lose sleep is, therefore,
to lose vital stamina, strength, health, and finally life itself. Hunger and thirst are thought to be the most painful modes of death;
but the ingenuity of despotism has, we are given to understand,
within a few years past, discovered one still more torturing—and
that is death by the loss of sleep. The helpless wretch is put
under the charge of cruel keepers, who never allow him, from the
date of his sentence, to close his eyes in slumber. He rages,
threatens, begs for death in any form—longs for impalement or any
active and violent form of torture—raves, blasphemes, and so at
last dies in agonies unspeakable.

Sleep a Force-Giver—Sleep is not only the tissue-builder,
but the force-giver. Our strength and alacrity for daily tasks,
whether of the mind or body, depend upon the quality and
amount of our daily sleep; and the amount and quality of the sleep
required depend not only upon the severity of those tasks, but
upon the perfection of the organism with which we pursue them.
The higher the capacity, the more and better is the sleep required.
Small and inactive brains, like small and inactive bodies, may perform their functions with much less rest than large and active ones.
The sleep required for health is in proportion to the physical and
mental strength of the individual. An erroneous notion prevails

that sleeplessness is an evidence of mind. It is simply an evidence of the want of mind, since those who have much mind must have a correspondingly large amount of sleep.

Regularity Essential—Now, it is essential to good and refreshing sleep that it be sound. A light and broken slumber, disturbed by vivid dreams in which the emotional and intellectual powers are generally abnormally active, does not answer the restoring purposes of nature; it neither builds nor strengthens the system; hence, refreshing sleep is necessarily sound. Again, it is a condition of sound sleep that it be regular—that is, that it should occupy pretty much the same hours in every day. Alternate sleeping and waking, during the same hours of successive days, has the effect, often if not commonly, of rendering sleep difficult, uneasy and insecure. On the whole, if late hours must often be kept, it is perhaps better that the hour of retiring should be uniformly late than occasionally and frequently late; though even this preferable method defeats the evident design of nature, as shown by the declining health of those who from some peculiar necessity of their occupation, habitually turn night into day and day into night. A few years of useless and hurtful fighting against a great law and they are worn out, and must yield and go back to natural habits or die. Thus we see that these four named conditions of good sleep are vitally connected; that sleep, to be refreshing, must be sound; that to be sound, it must be regular; and that to be regular it must be timely, or taken at those hours indicated by the order of nature and a once universal custom.

Injurious Effects of Fashionable Hours—In this respect of seasonable rest Nature has given way to Fashion. Fashionable society means late hours, and all who aspire to enter that charmed circle must conform to this requirement. The modern fine lady must not only have time for her elaborate toilet before making her appearance at any place of evening entertainment, but she must also postpone her arrival to such an hour that, the place being filled, she can attract the greatest number of admiring regards to the splendid elegance of her costume. So theatres, concerts, lectures and sermons must alike wait for her coming, since she it is who gives character and tone to all these assemblies. People who labor and who ought therefore to be in bed by nine or ten o'clock, P. M., must conform to this rule or forego all fashionable amusements, and therefore it is that they are urged by all the well disposed to forego these amusements. It is not that the entertainments are wrong in themselves, but they sin against the health and happiness of all workers, whether with brain or muscle, by trenching more and more deeply as time goes on upon the hours which Nature has consecrated to repose. If workingmen and women must have amusement—and we concede that they must and should—let them devise it for themselves, within seasonable and proper hours. A persistently and repeatedly broken sleep very soon produces mental derangement; and the directors of asylums for the insane have found, by experience, that regular and early hours are essential to the improvement of their patients and they require all their balls and parties to close punctually at ten o'clock, P. M. In this respect the insanity of fashion might well be placed under a like wise and judicious direction.

One hour of sleep in the early night is worth two at its end or in the day, for all the purpose of health and strength. If our ladies understood, what is undoubtedly the fact, that all their "beauty sleep" must be gained before 12 P. M., there would probably be fewer devotees of fashion among them. The faded, wan and prematurely old woman of society owe the earlier wreck of their once splendid charms more largely to irregular and untimely hours than perhaps to all other causes combined.

ALCOHOLIC LIQUORS

Alcoholic Liquor as a Cause of Disease—Those who die from the direct effect of intoxicating liquors—that is, of delirium tremens or drunkenness—comprise but a small portion of those who go down in their graves from this cause, for it is a fact well known to the medical profession that those who use stimulating liquors are far more liable to be attacked with any prevailing disease, and the fatality is also much greater in such cases, than with those of temperate habits. As a general rule, throughout the world, the first victims of cholera are drawn from those who use stimulants. The same is true in cases of sunstroke, chronic inflammation of the stomach, headache, diseases of the liver, jaundice, dropsy, impotency, gout, colic, peevish irritability, febrile diseases, epilepsy, apoplexy, loss of memory and mania. These are some of the diseases that afflict the rum drinker, and the habit is one of the most prolific causes known of lunacy. In England, Lord Shaftesbury, chairman of the commission on lunacy, stated in a parliamentary report that six out of every ten of the lunatics in their asylums are made so by the use of alcohol. Adulterated liquors in this country count their victims by the thousands. Wines said to be least injurious of the stimulants contain the adulterants in a very great degree. Many of them contain but little of the juice of the grape and some of them none at all. They are manufactured from dye-stuff, drugs and alcohol, with that most dangerous article, lead, added, to render them clear and prevent them becoming sour. Hence their use in any quantity can only be injurious to health and destructive to life.

Alcoholic Liquors Not Essential in Medicine—Dr. John Ellis of New York, says: "I can say that, after devoting over eighteen years to the study and practice of medicine, I have never seen eighteen cases in which the use of alcohol drinks have done my patients good. I have never seen a patient recover under their use, that I had not good reason to think would have recovered without them. I have frequently been called to see feeble persons, especially females, who had been taking wine, beer, brandy and the like for years, to strengthen them, and still they remained weak; and I have found that such patients improved when they were required to live on a proper diet and discontinue their stimulants. So far from being strengthened they had actually been debilitated by their use."

The celebrated Dr. Edmunds, of London, makes the following statement in his writings: "The cases in which I use alcohol in my practice I confess become less and less frequent every day. And I should feel that I lost very little were I deprived of it altogether." It is probable that there are conditions or states, in some few diseases, where stimulants of this character may do some good; but the great difficulty is to know exactly when this condition or state occurs, and there is usually more or less disagreement on this point among physicians. And when they do not effect good, they usually aggravate the disease and result in harm, for all undue excitement is necessarily followed by corresponding depression, and thus thousands are sent to a speedy grave in consequence of it. How can it be otherwise? Can a man who is prostrated to the very lowest ebb of life stand a course of stimulation whose reaction, all experience shows, will prostrate a well man? Take for example a most critical case, in which the patient is for days in a state where he can barely live without stimulants, and now let him be given these, and an unnatural state of excitement will follow, or a degree of activity above that which the exhausted organism is capable of sustaining; as a necessary consequence, corresponding depression must follow, and if the patient was barely at the living point before the prostration, which is sure to follow, he must now sink below that point. It may be asked, can not this state of excitement be kept up by the use of stimulants for days, until the patient recovers? If space would admit, we might logically show that this can rarely, if ever be done.

Alcoholic Liquors afford Neither Muscular Strength nor Nutriment—It is a law of the animal economy that any substance or food must, when taken into the body, be changed or decomposed into its elements before it can yield to the body those forces which produce muscular strength. Now the fact is, that when alcohol is taken into the body it leaves it again as alcohol undecomposed, there being no change wrought upon it. It therefore cannot have given up those elements that are needed in order to supply nutriment and muscular force. As an evidence that alcohol thus leaves the system undecomposed and without any change, you have but to give an individual a few tablespoonfuls and you can shortly afterwards smell its vapor as it is emitted from the pores of the skin. You can, as easily and definitely, reproduce and demonstrate the presence of alcohol by the exhalations from the skin and lungs, as you can the presence of arsenic in the body of a person who has been poisoned by it. Food is that which is decomposed in the body and supplies it with the forces which the body afterwards gives out. If your horse is tired by its journey, you can give him a feed of corn and time to digest it, and he goes into harness again as vigorous as ever and ready for the next stage. What is it that has taken him along through the second stage? It is the corn which has served as food to the animal, and has become decomposed in its tissues, just as the coal would be put into a locomotive furnace when the fire was going down. Now, suppose, instead of giving a horse a measure of corn, you give him a liberal allowance of whip, which is a stimulant? The horse goes on and works until more completely exhausted; and just so with a man. It should be recollected that food puts strength into a man by giving substance to supply waste; but alcoholic stimulants abstract strength from a man; they excite but to exhaust. Then recollect that when you employ stimulant, you are using that which will exhaust the last particle of strength with which your body otherwise would not part. That is what we always do when we work on stimulants; it is obviously unnatural, and therefore injurious. The foregoing statement being true—that alcoholic liquors furnish neither nutriment nor muscular strength—it must logically follow that their use is unnatural and injurious.

Alcohol an Enemy to Prosperity—To illustrate the beneficial effects that flow from curtailment of the use of alcoholic liquors, we give the following facts which were submitted by the clerk of the circuit court of Edwards County, in the State of Illinois, some time since:

"There has not been a licensed saloon in this county for over twenty-five years. During that time our jail has not averaged an occupant. This county never sent but one person to the penitentiary, and that man was sent up for killing his wife, while drunk on whisky obtained from a licensed saloon in an adjoining county.

"We have but very few paupers in our poor house, sometimes only three or four. Our taxes are thirty-two per cent. lower than they are in adjoining counties, where saloons are licensed. Our people are prosperous, peaceable and sober, there being very little drinking, except near Grayville, a licensed town of White County, near our border. The different terms of our circuit court occupy three or four days each year, and then the dockets are cleared."

Treatment of the Alcohol Habit—Dr. W. F. Waugh, of Philadelphia, has devoted considerable time to the study of the alcohol habit. In seeking the causes for the return of the drunkard to his habits of intoxication, he has noted the following:

"1. PREVIOUSLY EXISTING DISEASE which had led to drink. It is a misfortune to a neuralgic when the relief afforded by alcohol is manitested to him. Dyspepsia has caused many a man to become a drunkard.

"2. OVERWORK; especially when accompanied by ill-health. When a man begins to resort to alcohol to enable him to perform tasks which are above his unaided strength, he is calling the Saxons into Britain; he is invoking the aid of an ally who will certainly one day turn upon him with deadly effect. The most hopeless cases received in our asylums are those which come under this head.

"3 CATARRH OF THE STOMACH is responsible for many cases. This is due to the direct effect of alcohol upon the gastric mucous membrane. It is the source of the "next-morning headache," the thirst, and loathing of food in one who is just getting over a debauch. The temporary relief afforded by alcohol in these cases induces many to continue their potations who would otherwise have stopped.

"4. CATARRH OF THE MOUTH:—Although the gastric catarrh has been generally mentioned by writers, it is singular that none of them have called our attention to catarrh of the mouth. Observation shows that after a night's drinking there is great dryness of the mouth, the secretions of the mouth and salivary glands being suspended. I am convinced that in many cases the desire for drink has no deeper origin than the mouth.

"5. DEPRESSION:—The depression due to the withdrawal of the accustomed stimulus is, however, in nearly all cases, a powerful incentive to a relapse into habits of tippling.

"TREATMENT.—The treatment of these varieties must necessarily greatly vary. In the first and second classes the recognition of the cause affords the indication for treatment.

" In the third class, namely, that dependent on gastric catarrh, the following treatment has proved most beneficial in my hands: One hour before meals give a teacup of hot water in which has been dissolved ten grains of bicarbonate soda. This dissolves and carries off the tough adhesive mucus which coats the mucous membrane of the stomach, and which besides hindering digestion, acts also as a ferment. Half an hour later, drop upon the cleansed surface of the gastric mucous membrane, a small dose of subnitrate or subcarbonate of bismuth, oxide of zinc or oxide of silver. In a few days the catarrhal symptoms will subside. If the digestive fluids be not secreted in a healthy manner, minute doses of rhubarb and ipecac will restore the normal functions much more certainly than pepsin of any sort."

"In the fourth and fifth classes I desire to recommend the administration of Erythroxylon Coca. It is useless in the treatment of delirium tremens, but to relieve the depression resulting from the deprival of stimulants it has remarkable powers. Its effects in relieving one from the sense of fatigue are too well known to require more than a passing notice. I have frequently returned to

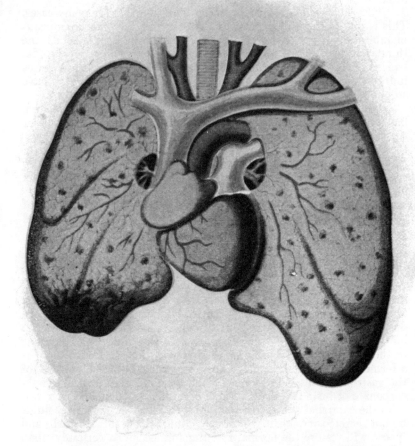

Lungs of Andrew Harper, who Died from the Effects of Cigarette Smoking.

The above illustration shows the shrunken condition of one of this young man's lungs, and the nicotine sediment in them. The lung is inflamed, and the nicotine shown in the dark spots.

Everyone should read the article on this subject in this book, after which it is not likely that he will ever do any more cigarette smoking.

my home after a hard day's work only to find that a still harder night awaited me in the shape of a tedious labor case. A dose of coca, however, removed the fatigue and left me as fresh as when starting out in the morning after a sound night's sleep."

Dr. Waugh proceeds to give instances of the alcohol habit cured by the use of the Erythroxylon Coca. To overcome the obstacle that men did not like to be seen taking medicine, he has put up the coca in masticatory plugs like tobacco, and called coca-bola. This has also had the additional effect of curing the tobacco chewing habit.

TOBACCO.

Tobacco a Poison—No one will question the fact that tobacco is a poison, who has observed the deadly sickness it usually produces when chewed or smoked by those not habituated to its use. There are but few substances in nature that are capable of destroying life so suddenly as tobacco. From one to two drops of the oil have frequently been administered to dogs and cats, and invariably in a few minutes life became extinct. Dr. Franklin applied the oily material which floats on the surface of water when a current of tobacco smoke is passed into it, to the tongue of a cat, and found it to destroy life in a few minutes.

Tobacco a Cause of Disease—Tobacco is a frequent cause of disease of the digestive organs, lungs, nervous system, head, eyes and brain. If causes heartburn, nausea and frequent belchings, pains and diseases of the liver; pains in the bowels, with disposition to diarrhea or costiveness. It causes, too, difficulty of breathing, oppression of the chest, pains in the chest, with inability to take in a long breath, and violent palpitation of the heart, as well as pain and stiffness of the back. Tobacco also produces a tendency to paralysis, causes drowsiness, unnatural sleep, nightmare, troublesome, anxious and frightful dreams, and a great number and variety of affections which we have not space to mention. In fact we have noticed but small proportion of the diseases which are asserted by some of our best medical writers to spring from the use of tobacco. Of course it affects different persons in different ways, searching out and seizing upon those parts of the body which are least able to resist its destructive force.

Yet there is seldom any one who habitually uses tobacco but will find himself troubled, more or less, by the symptoms of the above named diseases as soon as he stops its use; but while using it freely it will palliate or allay, as do all poisons, the symptoms its use has caused. Not infrequently on rising in the morning, after having abstained from its use during the night, he will get a slight glimpse of his waning vital energies; but his view will soon again be obscured when he partakes of the alluring leaf.

Medical Testimony—The senior physician to the Metro-
politan Free Hospital, in London, writes as follows: " I can testify,
from long observation, that the chronic use of tobacco in any form
is a very prevalent cause of debility and manifold diseases. Take,
first of all, the sense of sight: one of the most celebrated London
ophthalmic surgeons tells me that he is constantly consulted by
young gentlemen for weakness of vision, caused by smoking; and I
myself have in many cases seen the prolonged use of tobacco, especially when it is chewed, cause the total loss of sight. Then take
the circulatory system, and we find smokers subject to palpitation
of the heart and far less able to bear up against the extremes of
heat and cold than they were before making use of tobacco. The
use of tobacco is apt to cause a relaxation of the muscles of the back
of the mouth and dusky discoloration of the fauces, with hoarseness
from congestion of the vocal cords. The overwhelming majority
of cases of cancer of the lip are found in men who smoke, and cancer of the tongue has often been said to be caused by the irritation
of the fumes of the pipe or cigar. Great smokers lose, to some
extent, their vivacity; $i.\ e.,$ they are less vital than they used to be,
and less easily moved by a slight 'stimulus' which might be
pleasurable to non-smokers. They are notoriously dyspeptic. I
need hardly refer, indeed, to such a well known fact. They are
subject to constipation and ' malaise;' and when deprived of their
stimulus are more miserable, perhaps, than even drinkers. I must
take the liberty to protest against a custom which has been
inveighed against by Brodie, Copland, Critchett, Guerrin, Mante-
gazza, Cacopardo, and numerous heads of my profession in all
countries."

Mental Effects—Mr. Solly, an eminent writer on the brain,
said once in a clinical lecture on that frightful and formidable
malady, softening of the brain, " I would caution you as students
against the use of tobacco, and I would advise you to disabuse your
patients' minds of the idea that it is harmless. I have had a long
experience in brain-diseases, and I am satisfied now that smoking
is a most noxious habit. I know of no other cause or agent which
tends so much to bring on functional disease, and through this in
the end, to lead to organic diseases of the brain, as the excessive use
of tobacco."

The influence of tobacco on the human system is quite as much
to be dreaded as the use of alcoholic drinks. Drunkards invariably
are tobacco-users. Not one young man in a hundred would ever
think of using intoxicating liquors did he not first learn to use
tobacco in some form. Daughters of drunken fathers do not inherit
a hankering after spirituous liquors; neither would the sons, did
they but abstain from the use of tobacco. And yet ministers of
the gospel and many of the deacons of our churches, good men, so-
called, who preach temperance and cleanliness to the youths of the
land unceasingly, keep their mouths filled with the vile stuff or

make smoke-houses of their heads, as if the end and aim of life with them was to pickle their tongues in smoke; and their whole bodies are so saturated and polluted with the vile stuff that their neighbors' nostrils announce their coming afar off. Is it to be wondered at that so many of our young men, following in the steps of their illustrious fathers, learn to use tobacco and cultivate a taste for stimulants which at last becomes a direful disease and then finally die lunatics or drunkards?

The smoking of a single cigar, and especially by those not long habituated to its use, will increase the pulse from ten to fifteen beats. The results of both chewing and smoking often are depression of spirits, irritability, peevishness, loss of memory, dullness of perception and despondency, as a natural result of over-excitement. The teachers in our institution of learning not infrequently observe that young men who use tobacco, as a general rule, are much more dull and stupid than those who do not; and they, as well as eminent physicians, have expressed the opinion that tobacco to-day is doing almost as great a physical injury to the present generation as alcohol.

Sudden Death—Dr. Twitchell states that nearly all the cases of sudden death occurring during sleep, which came under his observation, were those of persons who had indulged largely in the use of tobacco. And subsequently the correctness of his statements was confirmed by investigations made by the Boston Society of Medical Observation.

Physical Effects—The use of tobacco produces marked alterations in the most expressive portions of the face. In consequence of the constant use of the muscles surrounding the mouth there is occasioned an irregular development of these parts, which presents a coarser appearance when compared with the rest of the features. The eye loses its natural fire and becomes dull and vacant, and the skin assumes a sallow appearance

Uncleanly—To say that this habit, with many, is uncleanly and even filthy, is only repeating what is expressed every day. The linen, the mouth, the breath, and many times the room of its victim, indicate the effect it produces.

Moral Effects—The use of tobacco has a tendency to impair the taste, so that simple fluid and simple diet are liable to become insipid and unpalatable, and the natural resort is then to the "flowing bowl." It also excites the various animal propensities beyond their proper balance, and tends to debase the moral character and make man more animal and less intellectual.

Expensive—Tobacco, in its different forms, costs the people of the United States $2,110,000,000 annually, all of which is far worse than if thrown away. It is not a natural food for man; it will not sustain life, but is a poison, and all its tendencies, except in rare cases, are to destroy life. Is it any wonder that we cry hard times, when there are hundreds of millions of dollars annually thrown away for tobacco and intoxicating beverages? Those who are so adroitly seeking for the cause of this condition of affairs, would they but take the trouble to examine the statistics and investigate this matter, would find herein one cause for this great depression that has been more potent than all others combined.

Cigarettes and Tobacco are Ruining Millions of Young Men and Boys, thereby developing the passions, softening and weakening the bones, and greatly injuring the brain and nervous system. A boy who early and freely uses tobacco never is known to make a man of much energy of character, and generally lacks mental and physical energy. The larger proportion of the aged, and those of mature years, very much lament that they were led to indulge in this habit. This should be a solemn warning to the young not to fall into the same error. Many boys have erroneously conceived the idea that to " puff " a cigar or cigarette, or chew a quid of tobacco, is manly—is genteel. Yet, if they did but know in what contempt such a course is held by the thoughtful and considerate, there would never be a repetition of it. I fancy I hear some young reader remark, " My father used tobacco many years, and died an old man; if tobacco killed him, it was very slow poison." I am apprised of the fact that some men of strong constitutions, active life and otherwise good habits, may use tobacco and alcohol, and even get drunk often, and yet live to a good old age; but they are exceptions to the general rule; a much greater number will die young.

Besides, it will be found that most of those who lived to an old age did not commence the use of these poisons very young; else they used them moderately and were never what we call hard drinkers or smokers. And we would further say to this young man, that if he were born after his father commenced using tobacco, he does not, for that very reason, if not for others, possess his father's strength of constitution, if the latter used tobacco as freely as most young men use it to-day; neither can he follow in his father's footsteps without the chances of filling a premature grave. How many of us are to-day suffering from paternal errors in consequence of the iniquities of fathers being visited on their children.

Tobacco Destroys Health, Imperils Social Standing, Extinguishes the Affections.—Besides it produces consumption, feeds dyspepsia, cherishes nervous diseases and palpitation of the heart, excites liver complaint, creates cancers, encourages headache, engenders weak eyes, invites disease and promotes softening of the brain. Its foul perfumes invade every railroad coach, street car and omnibus-line; contaminate hotels, boarding-houses and private apartments; its stench invades the family and social circle, and nauseates the mother, sickens the wife and insults the daughter; it extinguishes the affections of the doting lover, offends the young bride and disgusts the young maiden. It weakens the digestion, perverts the taste and leads to intemperance,

CIGARETTE CURE—(Anti-Cigarette League)

Mouth Wash, six ounces—Silver nitrate solution one eighth to one-fourth of one per cent.

Use a mouth wash after each meal, not to exceed three days, then after breakfast only for not more than four days. Do not swallow any of the solution.

Gentian Root (not the powder)—Chew a little whenever the desire for smoking appears. Gentian root is slightly tonic, and an aid to digestion. It may be used for several weeks without injury.

Diet—The diet for the first two weeks consists exclusively of fruits, well-baked cereal foods and milk. The best cereal foods are shredded wheat biscuits, corn flakes, puffed rice, puffed wheat, used with cream and milk. Whole wheat or rye bread may be used. The moderate use of nuts, well masticated, is of value. At the close of each meal use fresh sub-acid fruits, as peaches, pears, apples, pineapples. Sweet milk, buttermilk, malted milk, or cereal coffee may be used in place of coffee, tea, or cocoa.

While irritating and stimulating foods and drinks intensify the craving for narcotics, a grain-milk-fruit diet lessens it. In some special cases an entire milk diet for a few days may be beneficial; especially if there exists an irritable stomach bordering on ulceration, with an excess of hydrochloric acid. If the digestion is slow, and there is a deficiency or absence of free hydrochloric acid, a diet composed entirely of fresh fruits for a day or two preceding the grain-milk-fruit diet may be of benefit.

Eliminative baths, preferably the Turkish bath, will assist in rapidly getting rid of the stored-up nicotine. As a rule, it takes from three to six weeks to eliminate entirely the desire for tobacco. The time required depends upon how closely the directions are followed.

During the first few days, in the attempt to give up tobacco, the struggle is naturally the most trying. The Silver Nitrate solution and the Gentian root are valuable aids, both of which as stated, create a distaste for tobacco and making smoking undesirable. Being a metallic poison, the use of the Silver Nitrate solution should be continued only the first few days. By the end of the first week it will be recognized that the desire for tobacco has materially lessened. The consciousness that the desire is becoming less naturally begets confidence in the ability to conquer. After confidence is restored the battle is practically an easy one. Each week it will be found there will be a notable decrease of the craving, with a corresponding increase of confidence, determination and will power.

Tobacco Chewing—Tobacco chewing at first is a habit, later it becomes a disease. A habit is hard to break, but disease is harder still. Five years or more of tobacco using establishes tobacco disease, a hard master. There is no positive antidote. One plan is to gradually chew less and less, using a pinch of tea or coffee in the mouth as a substitute. Some use cinchona bark in same way; others, Canada snake root, or dried celery. Another remedy is calamus root. This list includes the principal things used as a substitute for tobacco. As tobacco is decreased the substitute can be decreased also, gradually tapering off both to a finish.

Diet—It is important in such treatment that fresh and dried fruit be used as much as possible. Tobacco users usually feel disinclined to eat fruit, or much of it. Orange peel is often a help as a tobacco cure. The drink should be plain water, or orange juice, diluted with water, and sweetened.

Bread, fruit, vegetables and water is the best diet treatment for chronic disease such as mentioned; if the diet is used long enough relief is almost certain. Many persons will get discouraged and fall back in the old table habits, thinking it's no use. Damage in old cases is repaired slowly, and only those who will "fight all summer" will win.

TOBACCO CURE

Treatment—Carry a box of one grain zinc sulpho-carbolate tablets, and when the desire to smoke comes on nibble one of these. They are harmless and produce a metallic taste.

Internal Treatment—Take a five-grain quinine pill before each meal, reducing the dose to two grains as soon as the tobacco craving passes away. Continue this for two weeks and then stop, resuming whenever there is a tendency to relapse.

Diet—Eat plenty of good nourishing food three times daily and lunch in between if hungry.

Exercise—Take plenty of active outdoor exercise (in work or recreation) to divert the mind as well as improve the general health. Be very regular in habits of daily life.

Tobacco chewers may use, in addition to the quinine treatment, some chewing gum to which a small amount of gentian root has been added. The patient should avoid, as far as possible, association and places where tobacco is used until the cure is well established.

VIGOROUS MANHOOD

To achieve vigorous manhood at least five qualities are necessary. One of these is *muscular strength,* the importance of which is realized by every man. But one may have strong muscles, and still be unable to use them to the best advantage in a race or in any contest requiring continued exertion, unless he also has *endurance.* A third necessary quality is *energy;* without it a young man will make but little headway in athletics, in study, or in business life. Two other important qualities are *courage* and *will-power;* these enable a man to become a valuable half-back in football, or to assume important positions of leadership in school and in business.

There are numerous examples of vigorous men in recent history and in present-day American life. Walter Johnson, the great pitcher, combines self-control and will-power with muscular strength, energy and endurance. He keeps in good condition by taking scrupulous care of his body. Modern baseball requires men who train and develop strong bodies and alert minds.
gave the world a wonderful record of endurance, energy, will-

Captain Robert F. Scott, who reached the South Pole in 1912, power, and courage.

When Livingston faced the dangers of fever, sunstroke, wild animals, and savages, and traveled 1,000 miles into the heart of Africa, all the qualities of vigorous manhood were necessary.

Lincoln, as a youth, could sink an ax deeper into a tree than any other man in the community. He could out-lift, out-work, and out-wrestle other men. He showed vigor of manhood.

How Vigorous Manhood Is Achieved—Those who would achieve the maximum vigor must observe at least five essentials. The first of these is sufficient exercise of the right kind. Reading the sporting page, yelling in the grandstand, and watching the baseball bulletin boards may be enjoyable, but will never make a man vigorous. He himself must take daily exercise. Hiking, baseball, rowing and canoeing, skating in the open air, swimming, if taken moderately, general gymnasium work, boxing and wrestling, where the air is fresh, are among the beneficial forms of exercise.

A young man's daily exercise should be vigorous enough to cause him to perspire freely. This helps his body to throw off certain waste products which would act as poisons if they were allowed to accumulate. After exercise a bath should be taken. A shower is better than a tub bath. A wash bowl or any contrivance is better than nothing. Warm water should be used first, then cold. The bath should be followed by a vigorous rub-down with a coarse towel, the whole process taking no longer than four or five minutes. The bath and rub-down should produce a healthy glow of the body and a general feeling of well-being.

Second, young men should sleep in the fresh air, work and exercise in the fresh air as much as possible, and be sure to have the indoor air kept fresh during the day. Fresh air is the one cure-all. It is usually more valuable than any quantity of medicine.

In the third place, most young men need at least eight hours' sleep every night, and most boys between the ages of thirteen and sixteen need from eight and one-half to nine and one-half hours. With less, one can get along, but he can not keep himself in the best possible physical condition. One should not lie in bed after waking up, but should jump out and dress immediately.

Proper food is another requirement. One should eat chiefly fresh vegetables, cereals (wheat, oatmeal, and rice), bread (preferably whole wheat bread) and butter, eggs and fruit, with fresh meat or fish not oftener than once a day. The system needs not only the kind of food that is rich in nutriment, but vegetables and other coarser food to give bulk and stimulate the action of the intestines. All food should be chewed to a pulp.

Not only is it necessary to eat wisely—it is also important to pass off the waste materials by regular movements of the bowels. When this is not done, one becomes constipated and is likely to have headaches and general ill health. Regular movements of the bowels are aided by the abundance of exercise and by eating plenty of fruit and drinking plenty of pure water.

The Relation of the Reproductive Organs to Vigor—Finally, if one is to win vigorous manhood and retain it, it is important that he should understand the relationship of the reproductive organs to vigor. This needs to be carefully explained, because, while the facts are important, they are not generally understood.

It would not be possible for a small, immature boy to achieve the full vigor of manhood were it not for the reproductive or sex organs. This fact may be made clear by referring to the activity of the various glands in the body. Most men are familiar with the salivary glands, and the glands in the stomach which secrete the gastric juice. There are also glands which make secretions that are absorbed by the blood. One of these glands, called the thyroid is in the neck. It is absolutely necessary for the blood to absorb the secretion of this gland. If a boy were seriously injured in the neck so as to necessitate the removal of the thyroid gland, he would probably become feeble-minded.

Horses also have thyroid glands and other glands which make secretions that are absorbed into the blood. Two of these glands hang from the outside of the body in a sack. They are the testicles (or balls). When a male colt is about one year old, these glands are generally removed. We say that the colt is "cut" or "altered" or "castrated." When this is done the colt becomes a gelding. When the colt is not altered it becomes a stallion. The stallion has larger muscles, a finer, stronger body, and more vigor. He becomes a finer horse because the secretion manufactured by the testicles becomes part of the blood, and aids in the development of strength and vigor,

In some Oriental countries, when slaves that can be easily managed are wanted for the king's palace, little boys are sometimes cut or castrated and are allowed to grow up without testicles. Their beards fail to grow, their voices do not change, and they are likely to become cowardly, tricky and indolent. They do not become men.

Every man and every boy has two glands, called testicles, which hang from the lower part of the body. They secrete an exceedingly important substance, which is absorbed into the blood; the blood carries this substance or secretion all through the body, into the muscle and into the brain. It gives tone to the muscle, power to the brain and strength to the nerves.

At about the age of thirteen, fourteen or fifteen years, and sometimes earlier or later, boys undergo many physical changes. The shoulders broaden, the height increases, the voice changes, the hair begins to grow coarser and longer on the face, under the arms and around the sex organs. These organs themselves (the scrotum or bag, the two testicles and the penis) increases in size at this time. All these changes are natural and are to be expected. If they occur as late as fifteen, sixteen or seventeen years of age, however, the boy should not worry. In some respects he has an advantage over the boy in whom they take place much earlier.

Seminal Emissions—Inside the body, near the bladder, are two other glands, called the seminal vesicles. When a youth reaches the age of fifteen, sixteen or seventeen (though it may be earlier or later), these glands becomes filled with a fluid which is occasionally discharged in the night. This discharge is called a seminal or nocturnal emission. It is a perfectly normal experience. It may come two, three or four times a month, or only once in two or three months. It is well not to lie on the back when sleeping, and well not to drink much water late in the evening. Lying on the back brings the bladder directly over the seminal vesicles. If the bladder is full, it may cause an irritation of the vesicles, with too frequent emissions as a result. If a boy or man permits himself to get in a state of continued sexual excitement by continually thinking of sexual matters, these experiences may happen so often as to be weakening. If he keeps himself clean in mind and body, however, and feels no ill effects from emissions, he need not and should not worry.

Knowing these facts, the young man will not permit himself to become the victim of quack doctors. In many cities unscrupulous men advertise to cure "lost manhood," "nervous debility," "pimples," and other things which have nothing to do with sexual health. They try to frighten the ignorant into paying large sums of money for the "cure" of diseases which do not exist. Many boys are bothered by pimples on the body when they reach the age of about fifteen, sixteen or seventeen. These are *not* an indication of any sexual disorder whatsoever, and they need cause no worry.

The Relation of Mind to Vigor—The condition of the mind also has considerable to do with vigor. Various mental conditions often cause bodily changes. For instance, sorrow, a mental condition, may cause loss of appetite. Embarrassments, a mental condition, may cause one to blush. Likewise, if a boy or man permits himself to look at suggestive pictures, to listen to vulgar stories, and to indulge in lewd thoughts, he brings about a mental condition which is likely to result in evil practices. While it is not always possible to prevent these things coming to one's attention, it is possible, by using one's will-power, to direct the attention away from these harmful influences and center it on wholesome subjects. Some young men will need to learn the trick of switching the thoughts away from suggestive subjects quickly to sports, school work, or other helpful activities. The mind should not be made a cesspool, but a reservoir.

Dangers to Manly Vigor—By faithful adherence to the five requirements previously mentioned, one develops a high degree of bodily resistance. By keeping one's self in prime condition all the time, tuberculosis, typhoid fever, grip, colds, diphtheria and many other diseases generally may be avoided.

It seems important, however, to refer in some detail to two diseases which are caused by the misuse of the reproductive organs, because many men do not understand how serious they are. These diseases are gonorrhea (or clap) and syphilis. They are caused by sexual intercourse with prostitutes (women who sell their bodies to gratify the lust of men). In general, it may be said that some prostitutes are diseased all the time, and all of them some of the time. Gonorrhea is often apparently cured in a few weeks' time, but the germs may remain in the body. Years afterward the disease may return and bring serious complications to the man himself, or he may give it to his wife. She may become an invalid for life, or give birth to a child who becomes blind a few hours after birth. Syphilis is in some respects worse. It may cause insanity or paralysis in the man himself, or terrible afflictions to his children. The only safe way to avoid venereal diseases is to keep away from prostitutes and loose girls. The widespread notion among the uninformed that gonorrhea is a mere annoyance, "no worse than a cold," is based entirely upon lamentable ignorance. It is absolutely false.

Venereal Diseases—Are in truth most powerful and persistent *enemies of efficiency*. A conservative estimate shows that these disease cost at least $300,000,000.00 a year in reduced efficiency. Three hundred million dollars a year.

And until the public and the vast army of employers realize how infected persons endanger the public interest, safety and health and do their utmost to prevent these diseases, this huge total of wasted resources will appear between the lines of every yearly budget.

PROTECT YOUR HOME

We have fire insurance and fire extinguishers to safeguard us against loss from fire. We have cyclone cellars and tornado insurance to protect us from loss by storm. We have police to safeguard us from burglars. And we use them all when it is necessary But we are not availing ourselves of the agencies at hand for the prevention and cure of social diseases. They are more destructive than all the devilish equipment of the recent WORLD WAR and continue on their stealthy way, destroying the innocent as ruthlessly as the guilty.

Lurking behind the protecting screen of ignorance, fear, timidity and false modesty, these assassins play no favorites. The mother in her home, the innocent little child, the untaught youth are all easy prey.

Now, listen!—There are going to be some older fellows who will come to you some day. Watch for this. They are going to come to you and they are going to tempt you and sing the song that every man has had sung in his ears—that sexual intercourse with women and girls is a necessary thing. Though some ignorant men hold that sexual intercourse is necessary to physical health, this is contrary to the best medical authority. A statement recently signed by 360 of the foremost medical men in the United States, including such noted men as Dr. Billings of Chicago, the Dr. Mayo brothers, of Rochester, Minn., Dr. Jacoby, Dr. J. B. Murphy of Chicago, and many others agreed against this old theory, declares that there is no evidence that abstinence from sex activity is "inconsistent with the highest physical, mental and moral efficiency." Men who act upon this false idea of sex often find out to their sorrow that sexual intercourse for them has resulted in disease and not health. When a prize fighter is training for a fight and needs all the vigor and endurance possible, his trainer insists upon abstinence from sexual activity.

While it is important for a youth to understand the facts herein stated, it is not necessary for him to remember all the details referred to. In fact, he should dismiss all these matters from his mind. The important thing for him to do is to lead an active, vigorous life, and nature, as a rule, will take excellent care of him.

Reproduction—The first function of the sex or reproductive organs is to develop the boy into a vigorous man. The other function is to enable him to reproduce himself when he becomes mature and the head of a family. By the process of reproduction, all forms of life—flowers, trees, birds, fish, wild and domestic animals, and human beings—are perpetuated on the earth. If the function of reproduction did not exist in life, the earth would soon become barren. Since reproduction is essential, it is important to understand how life is passed from one generation to another.

Reproduction in Plant Life—In many forms of plant life the flower contains the reproductive organs. In its center is a single organ called the pistil. Around it are several short stems, called stamens, on the top of which is the yellowish dust, or pollen. At the base of the pistil is a receptacle, called the ovary, in which are minute germ cells, called ova. Cells of a different kind develop from the pollen. The ova may be spoken of as the female cells, and the cells which develop from the pollen as the male cells. When the flower is in full bloom it is ready to do its part in reproducing the plant. As bees fly about from one plant to another they carry pollen from flower to flower. Part of this pollen is brushed off on the tops of the pistils. Germ cells from the pollen go down through the pistil into the ovary, where they fertilize the ova; that is, they make the ova capable of growing. After the ova are fertilized, they slowly develop into seeds. The upper part of the flower dies and drops away. The ovary becomes a seed pod, in which several fully matured seeds can be found. These may be kept through the winter.

Reproduction in Animal Life—The salmon of the Pacific ocean furnish interesting examples of reproduction in animal life. In the spring they swim into the rivers and find shallow, sheltered places for nests. There the female lays a large quantity of eggs. She then swims away and the male comes to the nest and deposits from his body a quantity of fertilizing fluid, containing cells called sperms. Thus they work back and forth until the female has laid several thousands of eggs. Many are fertilized by the sperms and develop into young fish. The male and the female, however, are exhausted by the process of reproduction. They drift down the stream in a helpless condition and very few ever reach the ocean alive. They give up their lives in producing their young.

Reproduction in Human Life—Human reproduction is similar in many ways to reproduction in the flower. Inside the human mother's body are minute germ cells called ova. In the male sex organs other minute germ cells, called sperms, develop. When a sperm cell comes in contact with an ovum inside of the mother's body, it fertilizes it, thus making it capable of growing. It slowly develops, being constantly protected by the mother's body and continually nourished by the blood from her heart. It slowly takes the form of a human being, until, after nine months of growth, it has sufficient strength to live without the direct protection of the mother's body, and then is born a new human life into the world. Both before and after birth the mother sacrifices much for the new life.

The Superiority of Man—Reproduction in plant life is largely dependent upon the action of bees, the wind and other natural forces. In animal life, reproduction is almost automatic. The salmon simply obey the reproduction instinct when the springtime comes. Man has the reproductive instinct, but he has acquired the power to control it to a far greater extent than have the animals.

The sex instinct may be a source of destruction or a great blessing. If it be abused, disease and suffering may result for the man and his wife and children. If it be understood and controlled, it becomes a source of added strength and a richer and fuller life. The nature of the sex instinct may be understood by comparing it with other forces in life. Fire is a great blessing to mankind. By means of it, machinery is made to perform gigantic tasks. It warms our houses and cooks our food. The warmth and glow of a campfire is a source of great pleasure to campers. When fire is controlled it is a valuable aid to man, but when it gets beyond control it may cause ruin.

The water above a dam becomes a source of power when directed into the turbines which run dynamos. If it be only held back by the dam, it may accumulate and cause a break, resulting in a flood. To be useful, it must not only be held back; it must also be directed.

So sex energy must be controlled and directed. The youth entering into manhood needs the full power of his will to keep his sex desires from leading him into practices that weaken and destroy himself and others. But the truer way of wisdom is in the preoccupation of the mind with healthful sex interests and the turning of the growing powers of youth into athletics, work, study, art, music, religion—any constructive social activity. Each of these looks out in one direction toward sex, and each gives opportunities for helpful relations with girls and women.

The Young Man's Relationship to Girls—The young man should think of all girls as the future mothers of the race, and understand that one of their most important functions in life is to become the mothers of healthy children who will make useful citizens. A nation may well be judged by its attitude toward women. The youth who is fair, will treat every girl as he expects others to treat his own sister.

In an accident at sea, when everyone is anxious to reach the lifeboats, the rule for all men is, "women and children first." If a man rushes in ahead of them, he is looked upon as a coward. It is more important for men to protect girls and women from other dangers, especially from those dangers which threaten to ruin their lives. Every man who has any principle believes in fair play. He despises cheating. The young man who is fair will adopt for his own life the same standard he demands of the woman he expects to marry some day. Each youth who grows up and marries becomes a link in a great chain of human beings. This chain reaches back into the past for thousands of years, and it may reach forward into the future for an even longer time. One false step may infect the racial stock and blight the lives of generations to come. If the young man keeps his body in good condition and lives a clean life, his descendants will in all probability be vigorous and useful citizens. The spark of life is to be accepted as a sacred trust to be transmitted undimmed to future generations.

Masturbation—Sometimes boys and young men are tempted to abuse the sex organs. If one, because of ignorance or weakness, makes this a practice, he runs the risk of missing the vigor he might otherwise achieve. Other serious effects are the weakening of the will-power and the loss of self-respect. If a boy or man who abuses himself stops immediately, once and for always, nature comes to his rescue and aids him in recovering self-respect, courage and vigor of mind and body. He can generally recover from any loss he may have suffered by a healthy, out-of-door life, with abundant exercise. To continue this habit will cause epilepsy, softening of the brain, insanity and moral imbecility. It makes the victim selfish, mean and contemptible in his whole physical appearance. If he persists in this demoralizing habit, he will have to be put in a straight jacket with his hands tied behind his back to prevent the inevitable result, which will speedily be insanity and death. The writer has visited many insane asylums throughout the United States and found out from the wardens that a majority of the inmates were there from this debasing vice. Many young men will laugh at this advice and warning now, but when older will mourn and regret their early indiscretions.

When this vile and debasing habit begins to show its effec⁺ upon the boy or young man, it not only destroys his health, but the mind and character. It affects his honor, ambition, energy, manhood, honesty, and veracity to such an extent that he cannot be relied upon, often complains of headache, gets weary at any exercise, pain in back, has cold, clammy hands, poor appetite, losing flesh, has poor digestion, heart becomes weak and palpitates, cannot sit erect and becomes flat chested; the lustre of the eye fades and he becomes pale, inability to study, nervous, bashful, timid, and often found alone; inclination to shun society; and sometimes the face is covered with blotches and pimples.

The foreskin of the sex organ should be in such a condition that one can draw it back when bathing and wash it clean. This will prevent the accumulation of an irritating, cheesy substance under the foreskin. If the condition of the organ prevents it thus being kept clean, circumcision may be resorted to upon the advice of the family physician. The youth should not worry if the sex organ becomes hard and erect at time. If he is wise he will pay no attention to this.

SELF-POLLUTION.

There are various names given to the unnatural and degrading vice of producing venereal excitement by the hand, or other means, generally resulting in a discharge of semen in the male and a corresponding emission in the female. Unfortunately, it is a vice by no means uncommon among the youth of both sexes, and is frequently continued into riper years.

Symptoms—The following are some of the symptoms of those who are addicted to the habit: Inclination to shun company or society; frequently being missed from the company of the family, or others with whom he or she is associated; becoming timid and bashful, and shunning the society of the opposite sex; the face is apt to be pale and often a bluish or purplish streak under the eyes, while the eyes themselves look dull and languid and the edges of the eyelids often become red and sore; the person can not look any one steadily in the face, but will drop the eyes or turn away from your gaze as if guilty of something mean.

The health soon becomes noticeably impaired; there will be general debility, a slowness of growth, weakness in the lower limbs, nervousness and unsteadiness of the hands, loss of memory, forgetfulness and inability to study or learn, a restless disposition, weak eyes and loss of sight, headache and inability to sleep, or wakefulness. Next come sore eyes, blindness, stupidity, consumption, spinal affection, emaciation, involuntary seminal emissions, loss of all energy or spirit, insanity and idiocy—the hopeless ruin of both body and mind. These latter results do not always follow. Yet they or some of them do often occur as the direct consequences of the pernicious habit.

The subject is an important one. Few, perhaps, ever think, or ever know, how many of the unfortunate inmates of our lunatic asylums have been sent there by this dreadful vice. Were the whole truth upon this subject known, it would alarm parents, as well as the guilty victims of the vice, more even than the dread of the cholera or small-pox.

Preventive Measures—When the parents are satisfied that their child is indulging in this habit, *take immediate measures to break it up.* It is a delicate matter for parents, especially for a father, to speak to his son about. It is different with the mother; she can more readily speak to a daughter upon subjects of that nature, and if guilty, portray to her the danger, the evil consequences and ruin which must result if the habit is not at once and forever abandoned. If persuasion and instruction will not do, other measures, such as will prove efficient, must be resorted to.

In case of a son, perhaps the better way will be for the services of the family physician to be engaged. He can portray to the misguided young man the horrors and evils of the habit in their bearing, and his caution and advice will have weight.

How to Detect and Prevent Secret Vice.—Examination of the linen is usually conclusive evidence in the case of boys; the genital organs, too, receive an undue share of attention. The patient should be constantly watched during the day until he falls asleep at night, and be required to arise directly he wakes in the morning. In confirmed cases the night-dress should be so arranged that the hands cannot touch the genital organs.

Under no circumstances should nurses ever be permitted unnecessarily *to handle or expose the genital organs of children*, and children should be taught at the very earliest period that it is immodest and even wrong, to handle the parts. When at school, as well as at home, *every boy should have a separate bed.* The neglect of this important advice is a frequent cause of bad habits being taught and practiced. In addition to a separate bed, he should be able to dress and *undress apart from the observation of others.* The necessary privacy may be secured by partitions placed between the beds, but not extending up to the ceiling, so as to interfere as little as possible with the ventilation. One of the few articles necessary in the sleeping room is a *sponge bath.* This, with a good-sized piece of honeycomb sponge, and a large towel or sheet, complete the outfit. The regular daily use of the sponge bath conduces greatly to the cure or prevention of self-abuse. The too free use of meat, highly-seasoned dishes, coffee, wine, late suppers, etc., strongly tend to excite animal propensities, which directly predispose to vice.

A Terrible Evil.—*In the City of Chicago in one school, an investigation proved that over sixty children under thirteen years of age were habitually practicing this degrading, health and life destroying habit, while among the older ones the habit was even worse, though not so easily detected.*

In a country school in Black Hawk Co., Iowa, one bad boy secretly taught all the rest until the entire school practiced this private vice during the noon hour when the teacher was away.

In New Orleans nearly all the pupils in a large female boarding school were practicing this horrible vice and the scandal of the fearful discovery is not yet forgotten.

Worth Millions.— *The foregoing article on self-abuse should be in the hands of every young person as it would be the means of saving many bright intellects from becoming stupid or imbeciles, or lunatics or from filling premature graves and be worth to them more than Astor's millions.*

D. S. BURTON

The above is an illustration of D. S. Burton of Harris, Pa., before the habits of secret vice had begun to tell on him.

The illustration on the following page shows the same young man three years later taken when he had become an inveterate victim of the vice.

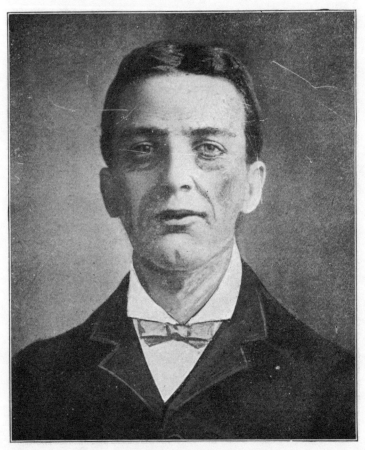

D. S. BURTON.

The doctor's opinion was: "If this young man escapes the asylum he and his parents will be fortunate."

The instructions in this volume will save many a young man from swelling the list of the unfortunate that are in the asylums all over the country.

DIVISION TWO.

IN THIS DIVISION OF THE BOOK ARE FULL INSTRUCTIONS HOW TO

KEEP OLD AGE MATTER OUT OF THE SYSTEM

AND

MAINTAIN, UNTIL A RIPE OLD AGE, THE APPEARANCE OF THOSE IN THE PRIME OF LIFE

Medical and scientific men now agree that this can be done to the 100-year limit, by following the instructions set forth, especially those on pages *64* and *65* of this book, and with it the means of prolonging life to a very great age.

The authors of this book give specific directions how WRINKLES may be avoided and OLD-AGE look prevented.

THOMAS PARR
Of Shropshire, England, Aged 152 Years 9 Months

HOW TO LIVE OVER 100 YEARS

Recent Discoveries.—Recent investigations have proved that nere and there persons have attained the ripe old age of from 125 to 185, one man in Hungary reaching the latter period. While these parties could rarely say by what means they attained such age, more recent discoveries and observations have plainly disclosed the way. By following the very simple method described on pages 64 and 65, almost anyone in ordinary health can add from 20 to 40 years to his life and live to be a centenarian and even more.

54

DON FRANCISCO GARCIA

One Hundred and Twelve Years Old, Resident of California

If people generally were informed by what simple means (recently discovered), most people could attain the age of 100 to 130 years or more, there would be almost a stampede in that direction.

BENJAMIN FRANKLIN

Benjamin Franklin's prescription for good health has never been surpassed. "Early to bed" is the first essential; simple food at regular hours the second, and exercise every day with not less than twenty-five deep breaths a day and four glasses of water, complete the prescription, which will bring renewed health and energy to any one who tries it and sticks to it. We can do so much for ourselves if we would but realize it.

METHUSELAH OF BIBLICAL FAME.

AGED 900 YEARS

Some people then knew how to live long.

We are just now learning how to prolong life.

THE LAW THAT ENABLED THESE MEN TO LIVE TO SUCH AD-VANCED AGES WILL DO THE SAME FOR THOUSANDS MORE.

THE LAWS OF CREATION ARE INEXORABLE. Why these men lived to such ripe ages, and how others may do the same.

SANDOW, THE GREAT MUSCULAR GIANT.

Scientists tell us that the causes of these strong men's premature death is "an impeded blood circulation, caused by coating and clogging of the blood vessels," rendering them easy victims of disease, and they die from what is termed "Heart Failure." When their blood vessels are kept cleared from these deposits, these strong men—and weaker ones, too—can live to a ripe old age, reaching 150 to 200 years or more.

WHY STRONG MEN DIE YOUNG

Strong Men Die Young—Persons with extraordinary muscular strength "strong men" certain products of "physical culture" manage to acquire over-development of certain groups of muscles, and certain professional athletes, trained by unwise trainers, are not only deficient in general health status as compared with ordinary persons, but are short lived. Excessive muscular development, overtraining, the freak development of the physical culture victim, does tax a man's heart and make him more vulnerable to purely mechanical failure of the heart in an emergency. Overgrown muscles sap a man's energy; they act as parasites on the body. Intelligent training does not seek, in fact, strives to avoid, hypertrophy, which is a great enlargement of the muscles of the body, or any of them, including the heart muscle itself; scientific training aims to develop freedom of movement, agility and endurance, not enormous strength. It is true that all athletic training involves a certain amount of overdevelopment of the right side of the heart, which pumps the blood to the lungs. When an athlete develops his "wind," or gets "second wind" that means that the right side of his heart has gained greater efficiency and is doing more work than it formerly could do without distress. A prominent physician states that it is for this reason that football should be prohibited in high school or other institutions for boys who are still growing rapidly, for such boys cannot safely train in a few weeks without seriously endangering their hearts, which are already taxed to keep pace with the rapid growth. Neither is a marathon race a proper thing for growing boys. A man's wind depends largely on the condition of his heart. When he finds himself growing quickly breathless, or short of breath on exertion, it is time for him to seek medical attention. Any one who cannot hold his breath while sitting at rest for forty seconds by the watch ought to visit his doctor for a general examination.

The Life Extension Institute has formulated sixteen rules of health.

There is so much said about the various things one must do to keep in good health that we are likely to become confused. It is therefore of great value to get the essentials boiled down into clear and concise shape.

1. Ventilate every room you occupy.
2. Wear light, loose and porous clothes.
3. Seek out-of-door occupations and recreations.
4. Sleep out, if you can.
5. Breathe deeply.
6. Avoid overeating and overweight.
7. Eat sparingly of meats and eggs.
8. Eat some hard, some bulky; some raw foods.
9. Eat slowly.

10. Use sufficient water internally and externally.
11. Evacuate thoroughly, regularly and frequently.
12. Do not allow poisons and infections to enter the body.
13. Stand, sit and walk erect.
14. Keep the teeth, gums and tongue clean.
15. Work, play, rest and sleep in moderation.
16. Keep serene.

Of course to get the most out of these words of advice they should be taken not as rules, but as principles; that is, they should be mixed with common sense and adapted to one's circumstances and physical condition.

Each of them is a generality, but it is well to keep in mind what someone said, to the effect that "all generalities are false, including this one."

One thing to be noted is that the observance of one or more of these rules is going to hurt a bit, is going to require some sacrifice, but a generality to which there is hardly an exception is that no good thing can be obtained without effort and self-sacrifice, and this holds particularly true in regard to health.

We may dodge the penalties of laziness, overindulgence and neglect almost anywhere else better than in regard to our bodies.

These bodies were made for vigor, for the forthputting of all their faculties.

And the brain in them was made to control the body.

We always pay the penalty when either of these functions fails.

Intelligent physical culture has very often brought one out of a state of illness into health, but it does something which is vastly more important than that; it keeps one in a state of health. When it comes to matters of bodily vigor, an ounce of prevention is worth a pound of cure.

WORDS OF PEARL

1st. Always stop eating with a good appetite.

2nd. When ailing, stop eating for a day or two and you will soon be well, in nine cases out of ten.

3rd. A mother should never be guilty of the reprehensible act of covering the face of her young infant, in doors or out. In the glaring sunlight shade its eyes.

4th. A mother should always teach her child to rinse out or wash out its mouth after each meal, which is as essential to cleanliness as washing of the table dishes.

5th. Chew each mouthful of food thoroughly and swallow it before another one is taken; in other words, eat slowly.

6th. People should never attend the banquet feast except when there is a natural demand; otherwise health is injured and life shortened. As a rule, people should sleep in separate beds. It is far more healthful.

HOW TO LIVE INDEFINITELY.

NEW SCIENCE OF SECURING PERFECT HEALTH AND HAPPINESS.
SICKNESS AND SORROW NEEDLESS WOES.

The Lord never intended that man should be sick any more than He wished him to starve. But He did not give him food directly nor perpetual health without effort. He did give him a fruitful earth and ability to make that earth yield food in plenty, and He did give him a mind wherewith to study and learn how to preserve his health indefinitely. Only mankind has worked so much harder to make the earth yield all sorts of material luxuries that he has neglected until these latter days to study his own power of getting well and keeping well. By mere accident some few have discovered this and that accounts for the miracles at shrines and at special resorts. It accounts too, for the real, though partial, success of the Christian Scientist, the Mind Healer, the Dowieite and others.

The truth as first fully promulgated by Harry Gaze of London, but also known, practiced and taught by several others both in this country and Europe, is that within each person lies dormant the power to cast out disease of all kinds and obtain perpetual health and full physical and mental strength and beauty.

The wise man of old said: "As a man thinketh in his heart so is he." If you permit no thought of disease and death to enter your mind you will have accomplished nine-tenths of the battle to stave off these foes. If you think you'll take cold you are ten times as apt to take cold as you are if you *think* you will not take cold. The other tenth lies in the simple safeguards of breathing plenty of fresh air and eating only suitable foods.

Each person needs at least 300 cubic feet of fresh air per hour to breathe. The air he breathes in supplies oxygen to burn up the refuse brought to the lungs. The air he breathes out contains the dead matter or waste. The body is constantly changing. The old idea was that the body is wholly renewed once in seven years, but according to Prof. Flammarion and other modern scientists, in a little less than one year the entire body, muscles, bones and all is renewed, all the old body having been in the meantime gradually consumed and discharged through the breath, the perspiration, the urine and the fæces. Hence it is absolutely necessary to keep these avenues of discharge acting fully and freely. Habits of breathing deeply and regularly, as you do naturally during sleep, should be formed. A good practice is to spend a few minutes every morning and evening in deep breathing, saying to yourself as you breathe in, "I'm taking in life," and when expelling the breath, "I'm breathing out death." For that is actually what you do. Tight clothing must of course be absolutely discarded.

Sufficient pure air taken into the lungs is an absolute specific against colds and pneumonia and is the greatest single factor in maintaining the blood pure. Impure blood is the cause of nearly all disease, for the natural powers will destroy disease germs that find their way into the system if the blood is pure.

Eating too much is the chief cause of impure blood, next is the eating of improper and improperly cooked food. Third is anger or violent thoughts of any kind, worry or depression. It has been scientifically demonstrated that anger poisons the blood both in men and in animals. Unwholesome thought as well as unwholesome food vitiates the blood The first step, therefore, toward attaining constant health is to form habits of right thoughts, the second to eat sparingly of proper food, third to breathe deeply of pure air.

Habits of right thought are formed by spending some time, ten minutes will help, an hour were better, in concentrating thought, the whole body at the time being relaxed. All thought is power, but calm, deliberate thought is most effective. Think of joy and a feeling of gladness steals over you. Think of health and you unconsciously begin to feel more comfortable, think of strength and you are already stronger.

As to food one needs to be guided by circumstances. Avoid sudden changes. Health and strength are promoted by avoiding meat but if accustomed to eating meat discard it little by little by substituting nuts, cheese and fruits.

No being possessing animal life subsists on cooked food, except man, and there is no being so unhealthy as man.

The ideal diet is nuts and fruits, preferably in the raw state, not green or overripe. This is known as the fruitarian diet that Adam and Eve lived on in the Garden of Eden. The vegetarian diet is intermediate between this and the animal diet. Vegetarian diet is better than animal but is not ideal, containing an excess of waste matter for the system to handle. Some people say they cannot eat fruit, but this is simply because they have taken it in connection with indigestible pastry or mixed with conflicting cream or sugar. Fruit should be eaten without either sugar or cream.

The ideal food for maintaining health and beauty, as already stated, is nuts and fruits as the exclusive diet. Prof. Gaze, while teaching classes all day and lecturing every evening at Los Angeles, Cal., lived for two months, January and February, on absolutely nothing else but nuts and ripe fruits. He took to this diet because he was then quite indisposed. At the end of the first month he found he had lost eight pounds in weight. At the end of the second month he found that he had regained the eight pounds in full and declared that he never felt better in all his life than at the end of those two months, nor had he ever had harder or more exacting work.

Exercise and activity are absolutely essential to life and health. It is a mistake to "retire" because of age. There is no "age," for the body is but little over one year old in any event and it is the thought that makes you become incapable.

Captain Diamond of San Francisco was 107 years old in 1903.

Yet he taught a class in physical culture and claimed to be able to walk 20 miles in a day without undue fatigue. At 70 he was an "old man," weak and near the end, according to the doctors. Then he learned of the power of thought and right eating and breathing and the result is apparent. A score of similar instances might be cited.

LIFE PROLONGED INDEFINITELY.

We know little of the life of early mankind, but we are reasonably sure that some lived to be 500 and up to 900 years of age. But the thought of death, on seeing earthly things die, hastened their end. Today, as ever since the earliest times, every child is born and reared and passes through life in the belief that in a little time he must sicken and die.

Man is endowed with two minds, the conscious and the subconscious. The latter preserves the activity of the vital organs when in sleep and when by accident or otherwise we are unconscious. But it is directly subject to the influences of the conscious mind, and if this holds steadily to the belief in gradual decay and death, the sub-conscious will gradually lessen its action and thus cause decay and death.

The new science teaches that if we can live from infancy, or better yet, prior to birth, by the unconscious power of the parents' thought, in the belief and expectancy of permanent life, then life can be maintained indefinitely by merely following the plan of life already outlined, a plan that will sustain the body by giving it only the food and drink necessary for renewal of the worn and waste particles without undue deposit of excess matter which clogs the natural channels of harmonious existence.

If the child is taught this belief and made acquainted with his natural powers of sustaining life indefinitely and grows up in a realization of the supreme influence of his thoughts and beliefs, there is no reason why he should not live forever as a human being in perfect health and with all his God-given capacity for enjoyment and happiness constantly retained, as the latest scientific investigations seem to prove.

Many imagine that to live the life that will give them perpetual health means that they must forego what they term the pleasures of life, but this everyone who has attained the higher life knows to be the opposite of the truth. In fact, the latest scientific study proves that the welfare of the body is best promoted, not by repression, but by proper expression of the normal physical appetites and desires. When we have cultivated right habits of thought and have all our passions and appetites under intelligent control, the pleasures of the physical nature are immeasurably prolonged and increased. Real joy and happiness are not attained through the isolation of the monk, nor yet through ignorant self-indulgence of abnormal or acquired tastes, but they do follow the self-discipline necessary to obtain full mentral control of bodily functions and the controlled expression of bodily appetites.

LIVE 75 YEARS AND 75 MORE.

After we have lived seventy-five years it is perfectly reasonable to add another seventy-five years in reasonable health and spirits. How to live a century and over is briefly told in the following paragraphs:

Oldest Men of Recent Authentic History.—Thomas Parr of Shropshire, England, lived to be 152 years and nine months old. Henry Jenkins of Yorkshire, England, died at the age of 169. John Rovin of Temesvar, Hungary, lived 172 years, his wife 164 years; Peter Zartin of the same place 185 years. Many in the United States attained ripe old ages, notably among whom was Henry Francisco of Whitehall, N. Y., who died in his 135th year.

Eminent scientists assert that man's body under favorable conditions may last 300 years or more.

The bones may endure for 4,000 years.
The lungs   "   "   "   1,500 years.
The skin   "   "   "   1,000 years.
The stomach, heart, liver, each 300 years, or more.
The kidneys 200 years, or more.

The principal reason why men become diseased or die sooner is because of the deposit of *animal soil* or of insoluble solids in the organs of life. Dissecting the body, as well as examination by the wonderful x-ray has proved the existence of these deposits in the arteries and veins, in the heart, the liver, the kidneys, the joints, &c. And how did these deposits get there? Almost exactly like the stony or chalky deposit gets on the bottom and sides of your old tea kettle. Look at it. The doctor says "There is ossification of the membranes and the patient cannot live." But *he can live if the cause* of this "ossification" is removed and something given that will gradually absorb and carry off these bony and stony deposits instead of all the time adding a little to them.

And Now the Remedy.—It is certainly the greatest as it is the simplest on earth. Every one knows that all water that touches the earth has taken up (absorbed) some solid impurities. You can, put two tablespoonfuls of salt in a glass brimful of water without the water running over if you do it slowly enough. Fresh rain water absorbs filth from the air and also from off the roof and is likewise contaminated. *When you drink the water that holds impurities or mineral solids suspended in it, these solids will as surely leave deposits in your system as they do in your tea kettle.* If you eat food cooked with such water you eat some of the stony matter. You can not escape it. Hence the cure must be found in taking out of the water all this injurious matter before you drink it or cook your food in it. This is done by distilling, done absolutely and fully. Science has proven also that distilled water has a wonderful power of absorbing mineral and animal solids, so that the constant use of pure (distilled) water will not only stop the further life-shortening deposits, but will gradually take up, absorb and carry off the deposits already in the system. For the water goes through the whole system. Drink a big draught on a hot day and you soon sweat out a goodly portion of it. It had to go all through the body to get from the stomach to the skin. This is the first part of the remedy.

Second part of the Remedy.—Pure water alone would not enable a person to live 200 years in good health. He must *avoid eating food which will leave deposits of animal soil around the kidneys.* Too much meat will do this. The system can use but a small proportion of nitrogen which is the chief food part of meat, the fiber is simply waste. If too much of this waste is taken into the stomach it begins slowly to deposit here and there some of this foul waste. The result after a time is disease caused by the slow poisoning from this deposit. Distilled water dissolves these deposits. So will the free use of ripe fruit, especially apples, peaches, grapes, oranges (the juice not the pulp), cherries, plums and berries.

Dr. Wm. Kinnear wrote as follows (*North American Review,* June, 1893):

"Very few people, it is safe to say, desire old age. We cannot defy death. But we may by searching, find certain secrets of nature and apply them to the renewal of the organs whose decay is constantly going on in the body. Anatomical experiment and investigation show that the chief characteristics of old age are deposits of earthy matter of a gelatinous and fibrinous character in the human system. Carbonate and phosphate of lime, mixed with other salts of a calcareous nature, have been found to furnish the greater part of these earthy deposits. Of course these earthy deposits, which affect all the physical organs, naturally interfere with their functions. Partial ossification of the heart produces the imperfect circulation of the blood, which affects the aged. When the arteries are clogged with calcareous matter there is interference with the circulation upon which nutrition depends. Without nutrition there is no repair of the body. Hence, G. H. Lewes states, that 'if the repair were always identical with the waste, life would only then be terminated by accident, *never by old age.*'

Paradoxical as it may sound, certain foods which we put into our mouths to preserve our lives, help at the same time to hurry us to the inevitable gate of the cemetery. A diet made up of fruit principally is best for people advancing in years, for the reason that being deficient in nitrogen the ossific deposits so much to be dreaded are more likely to be suspended. Moderate eaters have in all cases a much better chance of long life than those addicted to excesses of the table. Mr. De Lacy Evans, who made many careful researches in these regions of science, comes to the conclusion that fruits, fish and poultry, and young mutton and veal contain less of the earthy salts than other articles of food, and are therefore best for people. Beef and old mutton usually are overcharged with salts and should be avoided. If one desires to prolong life, therefore, it seems that moderate eating and a diet containing a minimum amount of earthy particles is most suitable to retard old age by preserving the system from blockages.

The powerful solvent properties of distilled water are well known. As carbonate of lime exists in nearly all drinking water, the careful distillation eliminates this harmful element. As a beverage, distilled water is rapidly absorbed into the blood; it keeps soluble those salts already in the blood and facilitates their excretion, thus preventing their undue deposit. The daily use of distilled water is, after middle life, one of the most important means of preventing secretion and the derangement of health. Hence, to sum up, the most rational modes of keeping physical decay or deterioration at bay, and thus retarding the approach of old age, are avoiding all foods rich in the earth salts, using much fruit, especially juicy, uncooked apples, and by taking *daily* two or three tumblerfuls of distilled water."

HISTORY AND WONDERS OF THE X-RAY

as here given should be read by everyone who wishes to keep up with the times. Its help in surgery and in locating internal disease is marvelous.

Genuineness of Precious Stones.—No imitation of gems, no matter how perfect in appearance, can possibly pass the scrutiny of the X-ray.

The X-ray will reveal, accurately, the contents of a trunk or satchel though these be locked and strapped ever so tightly. The would-be smuggler stands no chance of hiding his costly jewels or bric-a-bac from the scrutiny of the customs inspector armed with the X-ray.

Wonderful X-Ray.

In 1895 Prof. W. K. Roentgen, of Wurzberg, Germany, made a discovery of great importance to the medical world and of especial value in surgery. Shorn of all technical terms the discovery was simply that when an electric light was placed in a Crooke's tube (a big, long glass tube from which most of the air had been exhausted) some of the rays of light would pass through dense matter like clothing or wood or leather or flesh, and so light them up as to make these things transparent, that is, it enabled one to see the body through the clothes—to see the bones through the flesh. The light which easily penetrated clothing and flesh would not go through metal or bone. Thus a gloved hand exposed between this ray and a camera would produce a photograph (or skiagraph as it is called) of only the bones, the buttons on the glove and the rings that chanced to be on the finger. Expose the body, and a skiagraph would appear, showing clearly in the picture the internal bones and any irregular or improper piece of bone or any foreign substance of metal or glass or stone. The intervening flesh or clothing would not appear or appear only as an indefinite transparent haze. This Roentgen ray—or as it became generally known, the x-ray, because nobody knew what this peculiar ray of light is, and x is used in mathematics to represent the unknown or the to-be-found-out—this x-ray is rapidly coming into use to determine the presence in the body of sesamoid bones, or of foreign substances such as bullets or pins, needles or other things which may have been accidentally swallowed. It also shows clearly the position of a bone broken or crushed in an accident or otherwise. Shows whether it has been properly set, etc. and especially shows the exact condition of the joints.

Diamonds Detected.—Another use of the x-ray is in determining the genuineness of precious stones. Each gem casts its own peculiar shadow when a skiagraph or x-ray photograph of it is taken. Thus the pure diamond casts a faint translucent shadow. Any imitation diamond, no matter how perfectly made, throws a picture whose difference is at once apparent. It is much darker. No one could mistake it for an instant.

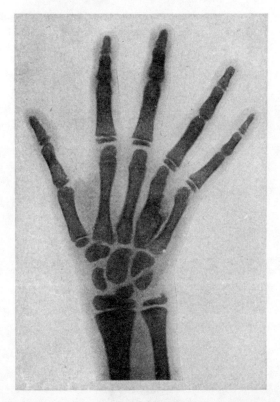

This is from án X-ray photograph of the hand of a son of a prominent physician in Chicago. The young man's hand was swollen and sore. The X-ray revealed the trouble as a growth upon the bones in the palm of the hand. Thus seen it was easily remedied.

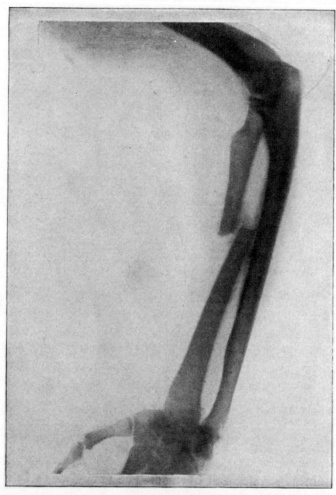

SKIAGRAPH OF THE ARM OF JAMES QUINN

It was so badly swollen when he reached the doctor that the possible break could not be located. The X-ray showed the surgeon exactly where the break was and enabled him to set it properly.

CHIROPRACTIC

It is a scientific method of adjusting the cause of disease without drugs or instruments and claims to be based on a correct knowledge of anatomy, especially the nervous system. The Chiropractic idea is that the cause of disease is in the person afflicted, and the adjustment in correcting the wrong that is producing it. The Chiropractic holds that the function of every organ in the body is controlled by mental impulses from the brain, which it transmits through the nerves. Any impigment of these nerves interfering with the transmission of mental impulses results in an abnormal function called disease. This interference is produced by subluxated vertebrae pressing upon nerves as they pass out from the spinal cord. The trained adjuster is able to locate the point of obstruction or interference and, by means of adjusting the subluxated vertebrae, corrects the cause, and normal condition.

The principles of Chiropractic was discovered and founded in 1895, by D. D. Palmer, of Davenport, Iowa, where the school is still located, and has had a wonderful growth.

Danger in the Ray.—In order to secure a "skiagraph" of any part of the body it is necessary to expose the parts for from one to ten minutes, or sometimes fifteen minutes, to the action of the light or x-ray. The person, of course, feels absolutely nothing of the effect of the light, which is perhaps two feet away and enclosed in a glass case. But in a week or so, especially after the longer exposure, the place sometimes becomes sore, showing all the effects of a deep burn. The sensation begins by an intense itching; it soon becomes red and inflamed or even blistered and is very sore and slow to heal. It was found, however, that by covering the skin over the place to be exposed to the x-ray with glycerine no "burn" resulted.

Diseased Organs Identified.—When an x-ray picture is taken the bones and foreign metallic, glass or stony articles, show clearly, but a shadow is also cast by the internal organs, and as these differ in density, their outlines may usually be determined. Whenever any organ is inflamed it will show a darker outline than normal. If enlarged it will be apparent. Thus fevers may be recognized, tumors located or rupture of the walls of an artery detected. By these means medical treatment which was based upon guess-work, often wrong, may be made positive, accurate and successful. If a clot is forming on the brain the x-ray will detect it and show the surgeon how to save the patient's life.

OBJECT LESSON OF THE EFFECT OF CIGARETTE SMOKING.

The fearful effects of cigarette smoking upon the stomach and lungs, as elsewhere illustrated, can scarcely be exaggerated. The analysis of the material composing the cigarette, made by prominent chemists and physicians, proves that opium, the extract of tonka beans (which contain a deadly poison), and other injurious substances invariably are used in the manufacture of an acceptable cigarette. What is known as "Havana flavoring" (tonka bean extract), is sold by the thousand barrels. The wrappers, which are popularly known as rice paper, are never made from rice, but, on the contrary, either from common paper, which makes the poorer grades, or from rag scrapings bleached white with arsenic, which makes the better grades. It is all cheap, but chemically foul and highly injurious. Cigarette smoking ruins the memories, the health and the morals of millions of boys throughout our country because of the sediment of poison which it deposits in the lungs and stomach and thence into the blood and brain.

Such eminent physicians as Sir Morell Mackenzie of London, England, Dr. Hammond, Dr. Sayre and others, have described such maladies as heart disease, cancer, epilepsy and insanity as directly due to the peculiar insidious poison from cigarettes.

A Healthy Stomach.

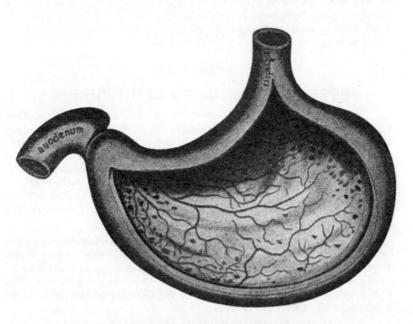

Inflamed Stomach of a Cigarette Smoker.

The use of cigarettes is ruining physically and mentally, **millions of boys.** Besides the danger of mental effects, the inflamed stomach is liable to give out before middle age. When a disease attacks a person of this kind, and it is more liable to than others, *their days are numbered.* **Every** young man should read the article on this subject in this book.

71

HOW TO SECURE HEALTH-PRESERVING BEDS.

One-third of your life time is spent in bed, and if that place is so conditioned as to cause sickness or disturbances in the body which will cause severe pain, rheumatic, neuralgic, etc., it is high time this were known and corrected.

The bed should be placed in a corner room or room having windows on two sides so as to secure perfect and free ventilation. The head of the bed should point to the north to secure the benefit of the magnetic currents that flow from the pole towards the equator.

The mattress should be of hair or of fresh straw, often renewed, or of excelsior. Feather mattresses are the worst. Feather covers are always dangerous, and if used should be thin and light weight. Heavy comforters are abominations and should be banished from civilized communities. All beds should be wide, the wider the better, especially if two occupy the same bed. On vacating the bed in the morning the covers should be thrown back and allowed to air for several hours, the longer the better. To make up the bed soon after it is vacated is to hold in its folds the poisonous gases that exuded from the body of the sleeper, and which are sure to contaminate the body of whoever next sleeps in that bed. Particles of putrid matter in the shape of gases have been known to lurk in such a bed for months. It need scarcely be added that strict cleanliness is absolutely necessary in order to keep the bed in a healthful condition.

PUTTING CHILDREN TO BED PROPERLY.

Foot Bath.—The first care of the mother should be to see that the child has a foot bath every night in warm weather and every second night or third night at other times. No woman who neglects this simple duty has a right to assume the rearing of a child. If the habit of the daily bath is formed from infancy it will seldom, if ever, be departed from in after life. Its value to the individual cannot be estimated in dollars and cents. Physiologists prove that it is more essential to keep the feet, especially the bottoms, clean than even the face.

Admit Pure and Expel Foul Air.—The next duty of the mother is to see that the windows are so arranged that one will admit fresh air all the time and another let out foul air. The bugbear of draught has laid the seeds of many a disease. It is a notorious fact that invalids camping out and sleeping out of doors and in the draft of a tent seldom or never take cold.

About the Covering.—Heavy bed covering should never go on a child's bed (or any one's bed). Thin single blankets or spreads, increased in number as the weather requires, are infinitely more healthful. Thick comforters are almost certain to prove too warm during the night and to be thrown or kicked off, resulting in a cold or cough.

CARE OF SKIN, COMPLEXION AND HAIR

To Beautify the Hands—To a wineglass of glycerine add the yolk of two eggs. Mix very thoroughly or rub in a mortar and bottle for use. No better preparation can be had for the hands.

For Whitening and Softening the Hands.—To one pint of cider vinegar add one ounce of saltpetre. This is one of the best preparations for the hands.

Brittle Nails—If the nails break easily, they should be soaked every night in slightly warm sweet almond or olive oil. The liquid may be put into a cup at a depth just sufficient to cover the finger tips. The same oil may be used several times. The soaking should be for ten minutes at least.

Hangnails—For a hangnail use collodion or new skin to coat the injury and give it a chance to heal.

Nail Biting—Both grown persons and children are aided in breaking the habit of biting their nails by dipping the finger tips in aloes. The following is also an excellent nail varnish for nail biters: Alcohol, 1¼ ounces; Chinoidin, ¼ ounce; Gum mastic, ¼ ounce; Gun myrrh, 1⅛ ounces. Mix. Let stand 48 hours, shaking the bottle occasionally. Apply with camel's hair brush. The preparation can be removed with either alcohol or hot water.

Nails are, as everyone knows, easily injured, and being so sensitive are very indicative of the person's state of health. A healthy person's nails grow quickly, and if the hands have never been abused or neglected, the nails grow out quite smooth and clear, showing the rosy skin underneath.

Ribbed or Ridged Nails—These are usually caused by a run-down system, old age, or sometimes by too much friction in polishing the nails. They can be cured if it is possible to find and remove the cause.

White Spots—White spots on the nails are generally caused from lack of care in manicuring. Be careful in pushing back the cuticle on the nail, that the air does not get under it. This removes the nourishment, and makes spots.

Sweaty Hands—For excessive sweating of the hands, paint the palms once or twice a week with a solution of ten grains of chromic acid in one ounce of water. This stains the skin yellow for a time. If that is objectionable, sponge the palms daily for a week with a solution of half an ounce of aluminum chlorid in two ounces of water. Or apply each night to the palms a pea-sized piece of the following ointment. Formalin, half a dram; menthol, two grains; lanolin, half an ounce; petrolatum, half an ounce. Or use a powder, once a day, for the hands made of boric acid, 98 per cent; salicylic acid, 2 per cent.

Ammonia for Hands—A drop or two of household ammonia in the water, when washing windows, dishes, etc., is very good.

Other remedies for chapped hands follow. Mutton suet 3 parts, lanolin, 6 parts, boric powder, 1 part. Melt suet and lanolin. Add boric powder, stir lightly until cool. Pour into moulds to harden.

MRS. C. L. CHASE
Aged Fifty-nine Years; Was a Resident of Tokyo, Japan,
for Twenty Years

THE SECRET OF BEAUTY

Mrs. Chase's face, at the age of fifty-nine years, was as smooth and free from wrinkles as at twenty-five. She used the simple Japanese method as given on page 76.

By use of this remarkable discovery every lady may regain the bloom of youth.

INDIAN CHIEF, BIG BEAR

This Indian chief at the age of eighty years had not a gray hair in his head. The simple remedy of grape vine as given on page 81 was used.

Salol allays inflammation through its antiseptic properties, and menthol allays itching, so the following combination is excellent for treating chapped hands: 1 part menthol, 2 parts salol, 2 parts olive oil, 60 parts lanolin. Warm lanolin slightly and work in other ingredients. Equal parts of camphor and glycerine will make hands smooth and white. Rub in thoroughly before retiring. In cases of persistent hardening, the following formula is recommended: Tincture of benzoin, 4 drams; alcohol, 6 ounces; water, 10 ounces.

WRINKLES, COMPLEXION, PORES

For Preventing and Removing Wrinkles—To prevent wrinkles apply sweet almond oil to the face once a week, rubbing it well into the skin. To remove wrinkles apply it two or three times a week. Use an upward movement in rubbing it in, and always apply just before retiring at night. The best way is to massage it in with the tips of the fingers. This stimulates the blood vessels to greater activity, which is very important. With his treatment, one should keep a smooth face until a ripe old age.

Cleansing Cream Formula—Two ounces of oil of sweet almonds; ½ ounce spermaceti; ½ ounce white wax; ½ ounce rose water; 20 grains powdered borax; and oil of rose, four drops.

Melt the spermaceti and white wax together at a moderate heat, add the oil of sweet almonds, stirring it thoroughly. Dissolve borax in rose water and add the mixture slowly. Beat briskly and thoroughly until cold. Add four drops oil of rose. The odor of the rose water evaporates in the beating, therefore the need of the oil of rose.

Be sure that you get oil of sweet almonds and not oil of peach stone or any other substitute which unscrupulous druggists may try to palm off on you. This cream is a light cream color.

I advise you to have this formula made up by a druggist, who has, of course, the necessary utensils, but if you do make it up yourself use a white porcelain dish and a wooden paddle to beat it.

Greaseless Cream—A good formula for a greaseless cream, which cleanses satisfactorily, however, is tragacanth, 80 grains; glycerine, ½ ounce; boric acid, ½ ounce; oil of bergamot, 5 drops; oil of rose, 1 drop; oil of lavender, 2 drops, and water enough to make one pint. Dissolve thoroughly with moderate heat. Apply freely to the hands and face, using some friction or massage, and then wipe off with a soft towel.

For Sallow Complexion—For a sallow complexion it is said that nothing is better than to eat freely of common garden carrots. One way to prepare them is to boil them to a pulp in a little water, mash and rub them through a colander or sieve in the water in which they were boiled. Then season to suit the taste, with salt and pepper and a little butter. Dilute with hot water until drinkable, and take as much as is desired every morning. As the vegetable is food and perfectly harmless, it may be used freely for some time, unless it disagrees with the digestion.

Enlarged Pores—The following lotion will correct large pores, but is especially recommended for oiliness of the skin. Orange flower water, 6 ounces; tincture of benzoin, ½ ounce; witch hazel, 2 ounces. Mix the witch hazel and the orange flower water, shake lightly, and add to the tincture of benzoin. Apply this wash with a piece of absorbent cotton, night and morning. If the face is very oily, wipe it off once or twice a day with diluted alcohol. For mild cases of oiliness of the skin, 1 dram of boric acid mixed with 4 ounces of rose water is helpful.

Madam Blake's Wrinkle Pomatum—This is the celebrated wrinkle remover that was always sold for a large price, and under a positive guarantee. With this formula ladies can make, at the cost of a few cents, what would cost them several dollars to buy at the stores, and which, many times, can not be had at all. Formula: Cocoanut oil, 1 ounce; sweet Almond oil, ¼ ounce. Mix. Apply to skin and rub in thoroughly. To prevent wrinkles use one ounce weekly. To remove wrinkles, apply two or three times a week. ALWAYS RUB UPWARD. For persons who have an oily skin, 10 drops of tincture of benzoin may be added before using. (Be careful not to mistake this for "benzine.")

Freckles,—To remove—1. Put grated horseradish into very sour milk, and let stand for 4 hours; then wash the face with it night and morning. Another remedy is the following: Lemon juice, 1 ounce; powdered borax, ¼ dram. Mix and let stand in a glass bottle for several days, then rub on the face and hands night and morning. Two teaspoonfuls of lemon juice equals one ounce.

2. For the light "summer freckles" use equal parts of glycerine and lemon juice. Or, if the skin is too tender to stand glycerine, rub a fresh slice of lemon over the face, letting the juice dry on and remain for a time. The following formula is also effective: Lactic acid, 4 ounces; glycerine, 2 ounces; rose water, 1 ounce.

Sunburn—A few minutes of exposure to the sun will cause blondes more trouble than it will brunettes by an hour's exposure. An old veteran, Dr. Brown of Kansas City, says that he always greased himself well before putting on his swimming togs. The skin of the face, shoulder, arms and legs will not blister nor burn if it is well greased before being exposed. Treat sunburn by applying cloths wrung out in soda water. If the skin is very much irritated, use a sterilized mixture of equal parts oil and lime water.

Chapping of Face and Hands—To prevent—A famous lotion for rough, red or chapped skin, such as women suffer from their housework, is make by boiling, stirring constantly and adding water to make up for evaporation, a pint of water containing three teaspoonfuls (three drams) of boric acid, about a tablespoonful (eighty grains) of tragacanth in shavings or chips, half an ounce, (tablespoonful) of glycerine, until a clear thin jelly is obtained. Apply a few drops to red, rough, chapped skin two or three times daily, preferably immediately after washing and before the skin is quite dry. This lotion is often grateful to relieve the irritation of the face after shaving. It may be scented with any perfume desired.

Rough Skin—This is an old formula, but an excellent one for keeping the skin smooth. Apply at night. Formula: Glycerine, 2 ounces; rose water, 2 ounces; bay rum, 2 ounces; carbolic acid, 5 drops.

Scotch Method for Removing Wrinkles—Sweet almond oil, 1 pint; best tar, 1 tablespoonful. Mix, and heat in a tin cup set in boiling water; stir until completely smooth. Add more oil if compound is too thick to run smoothly. Rub this on the face before going to bed; lay pieces of soft cloth on the cheeks and forehead to keep the tar from rubbing off. The bed linen may be protected by laying old sheets over the pillows. Wash off the application in the morning with warm water and soap. Repeat until the desired results is effected. This formula has been successfully used by hundreds. It also makes the skin smooth.

Complexion Wash—Add grated horseradish to sweet milk. Let stand one-half hour, and then apply with a soft cloth. Another good wash is made by adding a piece of gum-tolu the size of a nutmeg or larger to a small bowlful of soft water. After thirty minutes soaking, it is ready to use. A few applications will soften the skin, remove tan, and in many instances, freckles. This is much more valuable in beautifying the complexion than many of the costly cosmetics. Many of the latter penetrate the pores, and are injurious.

Excessive Perspiration—A person who suffers from excessive perspiration cannot keep themselves too clean. At least one entire warm bath a day is absolutely necessary, and several local ones. The axillae (arm pits) need the most careful attention, so do the feet. In the matter of shields and stockings, eternal vigilance is the watchword. A fresh pair of stockings should be put on every day, even if it necessitates a washing every night before one goes to bed. A good remedy for perspiration is to wash the armpits and feet night and morning in lukewarm water and castile soap; rinse well and dry. Then apply freely of the following solution: Alcohol, 1 pint; salicylic acid, 2 drams.

Body Odor—The disagreeable odor emanating from the skin is technically known as "bromidrosis" and is very hard to entirely overcome. For the feet (after washing as recommended below), use a powder consisting of powdered boric acid 95 per cent, and powdered salicylic acid 5 per cent, dusting into the shoes every morning. After bathing, a solution of 40 per cent formaldehyde, one teaspoonful to one pint of water should be applied lightly to all parts that sweat excessively. This solution may also be sprayed or gently applied to the feet. It is well to have several pairs of shoes, allowing those recently worn to be well aired.

Red Nose and Cheeks—Sometimes the face is too red because the skin is so very thin that the blood vessels beneath are too apparent, but usually the cause is impaired circulation or digestion. In the former case little can be done except to keep the face well powered as a protection when exposed to inclement weather, but under the latter conditions attention to diet and the wearing of loose enough clothing will help and the morning shower, outdoor exercise and deep breathing all conduce to the maintaining of a good complexion. Massage of the parts and application of spirits of camphor will help tone down a too high coloring.

Birthmarks, Moles, Scars—Afflictions such as these should be treated by a reputable skin specialist, and not hazard the face to possible permanent damage by incompetent operators.

Brown Spots—To remove brown spots, apply one to eight watery solution of hyposulphite of soda.

Face and Neck Bleach—There is a great deal of indiscretion among women in the use of bleaches. Never use on your face a bleach in which lead or mercury is used. Both of these ingredients are dangerously injurious. The following preparation has no harmful ingredients in it and it does effective work: Lactic acid, 1 fluid ounce; glycerine, 2 fluid ounces; tincture of benzoin, 2 fluid drams; and water enough to make 16 fluid ounces. If the skin shows slight irritation, discontinue for a day or two and use cold cream.

Dry Skin—If you are troubled with too dry a skin, use no more soap than is actually necessary for cleansing, substituting a good cold cream in its stead. Dry skin is prone to become wrinkled because the natural oil is lacking, so after the first coating of cream has been massaged into the skin and the face then dabbed and wiped clean with a soft cloth, put on a second coating of the cream every second night and let it stay on until morning. When about to be exposed to cold, wind or sun, rub in a little cream before applying this powder. This will help maintain the softness of the skin. Use a rice powder, or some brand of powder compounded for use on a dry skin, as this makes considerable difference.

Oily Skin—Rich, greasy foods must be substituted for a more wholesome diet.

The following lotion will also correct large pores, but it is especially recommended for oiliness of the skin: Orange flower water, 6 ounces; tincture of benzoin, ½ ounce; witch hazel, 2 ounces. Mix the witch hazel and the orange flower water, shake lightly and add to the tincture of benzoin. Apply this wash with a piece of absorbent cotton night and morning. If your face is very oily, wipe it off once or twice a day with diluted alcohol. For mild cases of oiliness of the skin, 1 dram of boracic acid mixed with four ounces of rose water is helpful.

Pimples, Blackheads—Every alternate night after a prolonged bathing with hot soap water and rinsing with hot, then cold water, sop on the skin with the fingers some of the following lotion, allowing it to dry on and washing off with tepid water next morning: Zinc sulphate, 1 dram; sulphrated potassium, 1 dram; rose water, 4 ounces. This is a mixture and should be shaken up well before using. Discontinue for a week or two if the skin becomes irritated.

Eyes, Care of—If there is no eye strain felt other than the natural tire after a day's work, there is no need of an eye wash.

However, it is a good practice, after the night washing to apply a warm cloth to the closed lids and letting it remain there a couple of minutes. This releases the eye muscles from the one set position they have been in, and rests them. Then in the morning, after bathing the face, repeat, using a cold water application to the closed lids. If the eyes are unusually tired or weak, then this wash is recommended: Boric acid, 1 per cent; sodium biborate, 1 gram; water camphor, 60 drops, and three ounces of distilled water. Apply with an eye cup.

French Remedy for Eyes—Bathe the eyes in cold water every morning on arising and every night before retiring. It is part of a French woman's religion to bathe her eyes. The cold water acts as a refreshing stimulant, and rests the nerve centers of the eyes, besides it cleanses the eye lids and eye lashes of specks of dust and germs which may be gathered there. It is a well known fact that very few women ever wear eye glasses in France. That is because they take good care of their eyes. As Lloyd George once said, during the Peace Conference, the "eyes have it."

Another good wash is boiled water in which a little salt—just enough to make the water taste salty—is used. The plain water will cause a smarting which the salt allays. It has the same effect as tears, the natural eye wash, which have a salty taste.

For tired eyes, a black silk handkerchief, or stocking, placed over the eyes will be found very restful when lying down during the day, or in lighted room at night.

Eyebrows and Eyelashes—With an eyebrow brush or a small, fine tooth brush, night and morning, brush your eyebrows to promote their gloss and train them into shape. If they are thin, rub yellow vaseline into them before brushing. Be very careful not to let any of the vaseline get into the eyes, as it is most irritating to them. Any ointment, in fact, used on the eyelashes and eyebrows must be applied with extreme care. The following tonic is excellent: Yellow vaseline, two ounces; oil of lavender, 15 drops, and oil of rosemary, 15 drops. Mix thoroughly. After you wash your face at night brush your eyebrows with a tiny brush upon which a few drops of the tonic have been placed. Particular pains must be taken if you apply this tonic to your eyelashes, as it will inflame the eyes, as any oil will, if it gets into them.

Hair, Care of—The hair should be brushed night and morning with a stiff bristle brush, using long even strokes, that do not jerk nor tear the hair, but remove dust and hair already loosened from the head. Many women with thick hair find most useful the brushes that have very stiff bristles in little clumps or groups on the brush instead of the brushes with bristles in great quantity, but wire brushes should never be used.

Shampoo the Hair with tincture of green soap. This is needed to restore the hair to a healthy condition. Any good quinine tonic is effective, or take: 1 ounce alcohol; 1 ounce distilled water; 1 ounce witch hazel; 50 grains of resorcin. Mix and massage into scalp nightly. Borax or a few drops of ammonia will cut the grease in the hair if added to the shampoo, but they also have a tendency to promote grayness.

Salt Treatment for Falling Hair—Take a basin of water (rain water, if you have it, if not, any kind), and put into it enough salt to make it quite briny. Take a cloth, dip it into the salt water and rub it well into the hair all around the edge. Then massage it well into the scalp with the fingers. Then part the hair, and with a wet cloth rub the salt water well into the entire scalp and massage as before. Allow the salt to stay on the hair about half an hour. Then take warm water and wash the hair and scalp thoroughly. Wash in several waters or until all the salt is out of the hair. Do this every ten days or two weeks. After three or four applications, the treatment usually proves successful.

You may use the salt brine, as above, without following by an immediate shampoo. Let the salt stay on all night and in the morning brush out every particle with a good vigorous brushing. This is particularly good in cases of oily hair. Repeat two or three nights before shampooing.

Hair—To Prevent Falling Out—Make a strong decoction of white oak bark in water and use it freely. It is best to make but little at time and have it fresh at least once a fortnight.

Gray Hair, to Prevent—Hulls of butternuts, 4 ounces; infuse in 1 quart of water one hour; add ½ ounce of copperas; apply with a soft brush every two or three days. When sea air turns hair gray, it should be kept oiled with some vegetable oil; not glycerine, as that combines with water too readily. The water that potatoes have been boiled in applied to the hair prevents grayness.

2. Sulphur, 1 ounce; bay rum, 4 ounces. Mix and apply to the scalp once a day.

3. Make a tea of the roots of common grape-vines, and wash the hair with it once a month. Some use it two or three times a month for a while when they discover a tendency to become gray. It is the method in use by the Indians. The root, or the bark of the root, of the grape-vine can usually be obtained at drug stores.

Superfluous Hair—For permanent relief nothing is as effective as the electric needle for the removal of superfluous hair, and where the superfluous hair is on the face, the electric needle is always recommended. However, a good depilatory may be applied to the arms or other parts of the body where it is desirable for superfluous hair to be removed. The following is one of the best depilatories: Sulphid of barium, 2 drams; oxide of zinc, 3 drams; starch, 3 drams. Mix these well and keep tightly corked. When you go to apply this depilatory, you add sufficient water to make a paste. This paste is then spread over the part and allowed to remain on for a couple of minutes. Then wash it off and apply cold cream, or soothing ointment. There will be resulting irritation. Generally you can tell when the paste has been on long enough by a slight burning sensation.

Peroxide of hydrogen may be used in milder cases. It bleaches the hair. It should be diluted with equal parts of water and the strength gradually increased. It is applied by using a piece of cotton wet with the solution. This must be repeated daily for a while until the desired result is obtained. An application of equal parts of peroxide and ammonia will bleach the hair first and after many applications tends to rot it.

Hair, Curly—A mixture that will help to keep the hair in curl is made by using 2 ounces gum arabic; 1 ounce salts of tartar; ¼ pint orange flower water; 1½ pint rose water. Mix thoroughly and tint with carmine if color is desired.

Curly Hair—To keep the crimp or curl in the hair, boil ¼ ounce of Iceland moss in a quart of water, and add a little rectified spirits to keep it. Perfume to suit.

Dandruff—A dandruff remedy that has been tried and found most successful in numerous cases is: 60 grains of sulphur mixed with 1 ounce of vaseline and applied every other night to the scalp with massage.

Powders—1.—Rose Perfumed Powder.—5 parts finest rice powder; 1 part oil of sandalwood; 1 part oil of rose. Mix ingredients, and if a pink tint is desired, add a small amount of the best carmine.
2. Face powder—Talcum powder, 15 ounces; starch 1½ ounces; orris root, 1½ ounces; oil of bergamot, 12 drops.

Blackheads—One of the principal characteristics of a bad skin is blackheads. Many remedies have been given for them, but one that is very excellent was recommended by a skin specialist. Apply a little gasoline to the face at the spots where the blackheads have appeared, patting it on with pieces of cotton. Allow the gasoline to remain for a short while and then rub vigorously with a turkish towel. Cleanse the face with warm water and good soap, thoroughly rinsing in cold water.

Pimples—For eruption or pimples on the face spread vaseline over the pimply part and then pat on as much sulphur as will stick, and let it remain for some hours.

Skin Invigorator—A good way to keep a firm smooth skin is by applying ice to the face every night and morning or very cold water. This treatment is also good for the throat and shoulders. Be sure, however, to dry the skin thoroughly and gently after the ice has been rubbed over it.

Red Ants—Red ants may be exterminated by washing every crevice of the room and cupboards with a strong solution of alum water. It will not injure the polish of the woodwork.

DIVISION THREE.

HOW TO SELECT A MATRIMONIAL PARTNER.

Perhaps no more important question can be raised by man or woman, who has arrived at a suitable age to enter upon the rights, duties, and responsibilities of married life, than the above.

To whom shall the young man or young lady apply for advice and counsel on this all important theme? They have some conception of the importance of the step; they recognize that to found a home, to transmit to posterity an image of themselves, to rear a brood of children and, so far as may be, to mould their characters and destinies for good, is a work of the highest significance, and who shall share with them this relationship and function is the question of questions.

Parental Advice.—It would seem only natural that the young should look to their parents for help and guidance in the matter, and what help parents can give is no doubt cheerfully given; but its value must depend upon the knowledge possessed by parents, and upon their ability to give disinterested advice. They have seen more of life and studied people more than their children.

The views herein presented on the subject of marriage vary from those commonly held, but, notwithstanding, they will be found invaluable both to parents and children.

There is such a faith in the overruling Providence of God as shall guide in answer to prayer in this matter, as in all others of human life, that will be adopted by many as the only safe protection against error.

Such persons deem their ignorance on all the many ramifications of the question a sufficient reason for passivity and say that, as a good wife or a good husband is the best gift that God can bestow, they will carefully watch the indications of His guidance and distrust their own judgment in favor of one bearing the tokens of being one sent from God.

Intuition.—There are others who, having simply determined that the one on whom they will bestow themselves shall be of suitable age, social standing, education and health, wait for that *intuition* that shall dawn upon them when in the presence of the affinity. They must feel, as a friend once said, "that jump of the heart" that was to him nature's infallible guide.

We shall not ridicule or quarrel with any opinions honestly entertained upon the subject, but will call attention to the fact that there is claimed for phrenology, joined with physiognomy, advantages possessed by no other theory bearing on this interesting question.

The Theory of Phrenology.—The theory underlying phrenology is that the real spiritual personalty, in clothing itself with a material covering for its temporal sojourn in this material world, has stamped its quality upon the body generally, and upon the covering of the brain specifically; that the appearance in general, and in particular of the head of man, gives an unerring guide to the inherent nature of the individual.

It claims, by long continued observation, to have acquired such a knowledge of these cranial protuberances and depressions as to grade them with exactness as to their location and degree or size, so that they may be read with accuracy by one schooled in the study.

If we need any apology for here introducing what phrenology has to say on the question, it is that nowhere else do we find any coherent teaching bearing upon it, and that, so far as we have examined the subject, phrenology has some strong points in its favor.

WHOM TO MARRY OR NOT TO MARRY.

One of the greatest causes of unhappiness, nay, misery, in the world, is the steady adherence to the superstition that two young people who feel, when in each other's company, the sexual excitement that is so often mistaken for love, must marry. It is folly for which thousands upon thousands are constantly paying a most fearful price. Love! Why, love means self sacrifice. It means wisdom. Many a man for love has remained a bachelor all his life.

Nature has decreed that certain dispositions will antagonize certain other dispositions. Marriage is often so hasty that these faulty dispositions are not discovered until after marriage, when it is too late to retreat, no matter how much it may be desired.

The following simple rules should be carefully studied and kept in mind.

1st. Two people of similar complexion and temperament should never marry. If they do it will prove a failure.

2nd. Two tall, slim people or two short, heavy-set people should not marry.

3rd. A nervous, fidgety person should never marry another nervous person.

4th. A man should never marry a woman who is given to finding fault, or who is peevish and "cranky," or who scolds her little brothers and sisters.

5th. A woman should never marry a man who is naturally inclined to be arrogant and cruel, or who is inordinately selfish.

6th. A man should never marry a woman who is so proud that she keeps her parents poor dressing and providing for her. Beauty never atones for pride.

7th. A man should never marry a woman who is "touchy" or fickle in her friendship, or often at "outs" with her parents. Depend upon it these characteristics are due to a serious fault in her nature which, after marriage, will reappear in her own home to make it miserable.

CHARACTERISTICS THAT ARE FATAL TO FUTURE HAPPINESS.

Some young men act very foolish in choosing a companion for life. They are apt to mistake a physical passion for love, and marry a girl who can never be a mate, because nature has decreed otherwise. Some think they fall in love with hair, or with eyes, or with dimples, or with a pretty figure. Temperament cuts a vastly greater figure than face. A pretty face with peevish or selfish temper is like a fair-skinned apple that is wormy or rotten within.

Don't marry a girl whose chief aim in life is dress; who hangs around dry goods or millinery stores like butterflies around a gorgeous flower.

To dress extravagantly is a blot upon any woman's character. When the activity of the mind is taken up with finery the soul grows pinched and lean, the mind fails to develop, and such a woman cannot make a decent partner for any sensible man.

So, too, should no girl think of accepting any young man for a lover

who is addicted to the use of liquor, or who spends his money in speculation or in fast living. Shun such as you would an idiot or a fool.
They will invariably prove worthless husbands, and to think that you
can reform them is so much like playing with fire that we must quote
old man Weller's advice to his son:

"Samivel—don't."

As it is to-day, in five homes out of six, domestic infelicity exists
merely because before marriage these fundamental points or elements
necessary to continued affection and happiness were disregarded.

LOOK BEFORE YOU LEAP INTO THE SEA OF MATRIMONY.

To select the characteristics that cause future trouble, while courting
one need only watch with some care how his intended treats her family
and friends. If she is cross to the dog, and the cat is afraid of her,
have a care; some day you may find yourself leading a dog's life.
Observe her conduct when she does not know you are observing her,
and judge her by the characteristics you thus discover.

To live as happily and continue as affectionate after marriage as
before is worth a little sacrifice, and it requires but very little sacrifice
if you go about it the right way. First, of course, you must continue
true to one another, but the secret will generally be found in one of two
things. The most important of these is the keeping alive and at its
best the sexual desires. This is the highest part of your nature and
should be held sacred. Constant or uninterrupted indulgence is sure to
destroy its enjoyment and destroy happiness for both.

The animals enforce periods of abstinence by instinct. Man has
sense instead of instinct, and if he fails to use his intelligence he suffers. It is absolutely necessary, if you retain affection, to separate indulgence with long periods of abstinence. It is on this rock that more
domestic happiness is ruined than on any other. And while it may
seem at first to be a sacrifice you will soon learn that it is instead a
means of adding exquisite pleasure to both your lives that you were
formerly strangers to.

LITTLE ACTS THAT WAKEN THE SMOULDERING LAMES OF LOVE.

Another important secret is in retaining all along the trifling acts of
tenderness. Young man, squeeze your wife's hand now and then after
marriage just as you did while courting, and look your wife in the eye
as you did then. And wife, pet your husband now and then ; think to
do it These may be trifles which many married folks will pooh-pooh
as beneath their dignity, but we have always found that such people
missed domestic happiness while the others retained it. Put away that
selfish unhappiness and begin to attend to these little acts of affection,
and if you continue it honestly for a little while you will be wonderfully
surprised at the prompt response. It will repay a thousand fold for
the effort.

HOW TO MAKE DOMESTIC HAPPINESS CONTINUOUS.

The glamour of youth pictures for love an eternal paradise of happiness in the association of the two who love each other. True, thus it should be, and in many instances it is so. In the majority of families, however, domestic happiness all too soon disappears. It is therefore of the utmost importance for the youthful couple that the rules which govern harmony be understood and lived up to.

WHEN PASSION SHOULD BE CURBED.

A man must not let his passion become selfish, and demand what a woman cannot and should not give. The man must bear in mind that while he is always passionate a woman's constitution differs and can properly meet him only periodically. For a man to demand more, or not to respect at all times the wife's nature in this respect, is to cause her to feel loathing toward him in spite of herself. The wife, on the other hand, should also recognize the reasonable need of her husband's natural desires, and while restraining indulgence with proper periods of rest, which vary according to conditions, from two weeks to two months, or longer, should not be niggardly. During pregnancy, with the possible exception of the last month, no true man will ever think of such indulgence. Mutual respect and affection are often sacrificed at this time by the husband's unreasonable demands.

WHEN SEPARATE APARTMENTS ARE NECESSARY.

A terrible strain upon the continued attraction of one for the other is the constant occupation of the same apartments. Few indeed can stand this. Young man, if you want your wife to be as attractive in your sight and as loving toward you all the time after marriage as before, see to it that you occupy separate apartments most of the time. It always pays richly for all that it costs in the way of temporary sacrifice.

Mutual forbearance with the special peculiarities of temper or preference is essential. The greatest obstacle to harmony is selfishness. If one will only think first of the happiness of the other under all circumstances, he will get more, enjoy more and live more than he ever can by trying to enforce his own way.

MONEY MATTERS A SOURCE OF UNHAPPINESS.

Money matters are the source of much discord and grief to both husband and wife. Man and wife are partners and are entitled to one-half of the common fund and no more. There is no sense in the woman begging for a little money from her husband, emphasizing thus her dependence upon his pleasure. While she is bearing children she is entitled to good pay for her services. Otherwise she should be independent of the man's liberality or stinginess, as the case may be, and earn her own money to spend for her own uses. There are a hundred ways in which she can do this, and the sense of independence that follows repays her for whatever social sacrifice it may entail.

DRESS A SOURCE OF HAPPINESS OR UNHAPPINESS.

Many otherwise happy families have been broken up through the wife's thoughtless extravagance in the matter of dress. In thousands of families, comparatively poor, the husband buys few clothes, in fact goes shabby, and buys only cheap garments; partly because his wife insists upon wearing showy gowns and bonnets beyond the family resources, sensibly utilized. It is sense to dress well—as well as your purse can afford, but it is nonsense and folly to go beyond that, just because some neighbor can afford a little more.

LECTURE TO GIRLS.

BY PROF. L. A. STANDISH, OF NEW YORK.

REWARDS OF VIRTUE.

If children were always born under perfect conditions and with a proper inheritance on both sides of the family for many generations back, and further, if the early environments were always what they should be, children when they grow up would be inclined to do only what is right and proper. But we all know there is not one in ten thousand that is so marvelously fortunate. Neither tne parents nor the children have any control over the influence of heredity, nor have they control over the early environments. Therefore it is that children as they grow up are so often inclined to yield to temptation and depart from the paths along which, and only along which, real happiness can be found.

There is no more awful hell of suffering on earth than the pangs of remorse from which you can never escape for one instant, while on the other hand, there is no joy so constant and so exhilarating as is the sense of satisfaction—of pleasure that comes from a clear conscience. Besides, all who have had experience, no matter what their age, will unite and do unite in declaring that a great amount of misery always follows a small amount of pleasure secured through forbidden paths.

The old saying that "virtue is its own reward" would be more nearly true if changed to "virtue brings its own reward." What, after all, is the greatest boon that can come to any one? Wealth? No. Fame? No. Pleasure? No. It is none of these. It is the good opinion of our fellows. The love of those with whom we associate. If we have that it gives us more pleasure, more real happiness than all else put together. Then is it not the part of wisdom to seek, to desire, to so order our lives, to so conduct ourselves, as to gain this good opinion of others—this love of our immediate companions?

And believe me, girls and boys, too, for that matter, there never yet in all the world's history, has been found one single instance where this-thing-so-much-to-be-desired was obtained through a departure from the ways of virtue and rectitude. You yourself cannot, if you try, love for any great length of time a companion who is mean or who cheats or who sells any part of his or her character for temporary pleas-

Prof. L. H. Standish

LECTURE TO GIRLS

On rewards of virtue.

On waywardness—evils that beset the wayward.

On the first wrong step.

On bitter toils of fallen life.

J. G. HOLLAND

LECTURE TO BOYS AND YOUNG MEN

On the rewards of honesty.
On the advantage of truth and veracity.
On how to determine a suitable occupation.
On evil effects of intemperance and profanity.
On injurious results from the use of tobacco.
On industry and economy the highway to wealth and fame.

are. You cannot do it. It is contrary to the laws of nature, which are the laws of God. But on the other hand it is easy to love an acquaintance whom we learn to feel we can trust perfectly ; we know that they will always do what is right in all times of trial—we say that we know it simply because we feel it, and we *feel* it simply because the other party by really *being* so *in her heart* causes th feeling. This is indeed one of the clearest examples of instinct among human beings. The feeling never comes and never stays unless the other party is really *true at heart.* You see God has made it a law of our bein that all the best things—the things everybody agrees on as being the most desirable things—come as a reward of virtue.

WAYWARDNESS.

Above Niagara there is a portion of the river where the water seems as smooth as glass. On a warm summer evening one is tempted to drop the oars and let the boat drift as it will. Danger would never enter the mind of any unwary voyager who had had n experience of the angry waters below. But any one thus drifting is likely to hear a voice from the shore.

"Boat ahoy! Aho-o-y!"

"What is it?"

"The rapids are below you. Pull for the shore!" And woe betide the fool hardy ones who heed not the friendly call. For though the water is so calm and the boat seems to lie so still it is slowly but surely being sucked by the undertow toward the rapids. Once upon these and his pulling is in vain. His doom is sealed.

How very like this is the fate of the young girl, who, to gratify a longing for excitement perhaps, or out of pure abandon, neglects the good advice of her mother and allows herself to float upon the giddy stream of error. She is not bad, would not be for the world. The mere suggestion of a shameful act would cause her anger. Never would she be guilty of that, "Only a little wayward," say her friends. Ah; could she only see the future and catch a glimpse of the pitfalls and the mire that lay a little further on along the path she is pursuing, how quickly she would stop. But she is drifting toward the Niagara where so many thousand every year made shipwreck of their young pure lives.

THE FIRST WRONG STEP.

It is so like youth to say, "Oh, pshaw! I'll quit in time enough! Don't you fear for me! I'm just having a little fun, but I shan't run into danger. I'm all right!" etc. If it were only so. Innocent and trusting youth! She knows not that the tempter will always take her unawares and she will never *never* recognize him till it is too late. Would it were otherwise. But so it has been since mother Eve dwelt in the garden and will always be till the millenium. The only time that you can safely stop is before you take the first step. It is easy then to say no and to fall back upon your native purity and pray, "God keep me beautiful within."

After the first wrong step the next is so much more natural. It does not seem so bad after all. There is no use in mamma being so strict anyhow. Well you are on the glassy still water just above the rapids now. How long will it be till your boat strikes the rapids? That no one can say. It may be years, it may be months, it may be only days. But when you are caught, God pity you.

BITTER TOILS OF FALLEN LIFE.

The writer once knew a beautiful woman—when he first met her she accidentally ran against him on a lonely walk on the river bank of a Missouri town. She was beautiful, in face and form, but an oath escaped her lips in reply to the "pardon me"—she was only 23. A year later in a tent on the banks of the same river he saw her die in pain from the effects of a loathsome disease contracted amid the shame that our cities license and permit. He had tried before, in vain, to help her forsake her fallen course. Now she was thankful to receive one kind word. She had been the petted favorite of the haunts of vice, now forsaken by all, and to me, a stranger, on her deathbed she told what a hell had been in her heart during all the time. Scarcely a moment's animal pleasure, but what was haunted by a mental woe within. And oh the heartaches when by herself alone. "And then" she said, her voice broken by sobs, "it was torture all the way. As a girl I was a little wayward—I liked to have a good time—I went with him some—he was such a nice boy, so were some of the others and we were only having a good time—of course, mother tried to stop it all and finally I ran away—I can't—I can't tell it—I'm too weak—it didn't come out as I expected—it's all misery." And with the cry "I'm lost" she died.

It is fortunate for the world that the maker of us all has put in our hearts a little monitor whom we can never escape. We can sometimes escape from foes and run to friends, but our own consciousness becomes a foe when we have done wrong and we cannot escape from it.

LECTURE TO BOYS AND YOUNG MEN.

BY J. G. HOLLAND

Many years ago P. T. Barnum, the noted showman, traveled throughout the United States giving lectures on "Success in Life and How to Make Money." In the course of these lectures he emphasized the three great essentials to a young man starting in life as *vocation*, *location* and *honesty*. Ability was an advantage, but he declared, and the declaration is proven by experience, that boys lacking any marked ability but following along the lines suggested, won far greater success, than brilliant, smart boys who followed their inclinations, or were induced to go in paths contrary to the teachings of experience.

REWARDS OF HONESTY.

A ragged newsboy in Chicago whose route lay along Wabash avenue, was handed a dime one evening for his paper. He had no change. but the man wanted the paper. "I'll git ye the charge, Mister," he said. "All right," said the customer, as he went back into the parlor. But when half an hour later no change had been brought he gave up his confidence in that boy's honesty. But just as he was about to retire, nearly ten o'clock, there came a ring at the door-bell. Going to the door he found a diminutive youngster who held up a little hand with nine pennies in it and a piping voice said: "Here, Mister, is yer change. Bob he got run over by de cars, and dey bring him home in der perlice wagon, and he say he was bringing de man his change, and he could not rest and could not stand it till 'de money was brung, so I brung it." The gentleman took the change and asked the boy's address. Next day, calling at the dingy back rooms where the little fellow said he lived, he found the boy to whom he had given the dime lying in his little cheap bed, out of his head, and moaning now and then, "Tim, Tim, you must git the change for the man; I said I would, and he'll think I stole it." The gentleman learned that the boy, while on the way back to return the change, was run down by a car unnoticed and found a little later by a policeman. The gentleman sent his own physician to attend the boy, who finally recovered, and after that paid his poor widowed mother enough to enable her to keep the boy in school and start him in an honorable business career.

We put honesty first, because it is more important than any other one thing in order to get on in the world. Too much has been said about shrewd traffic—about getting the better of your fellows. But there is nothing that stands more in the way of winning success in life than the meanness that comes from dishonest practices—and by dishonest practices we mean not alone taking something that don't belong to you—violating the law of the land—but any act of unfairness toward others. It is just as dishonest to fail to give what you know you ought to give as it is to steal. It is just as dishonest to live beyond your means, or to speculate with borrowed money, or to keep what you find and can find an owner for, as it is to break into a house and rob; and every dishonest act will make a smaller man of you, less capable, less thought of, less free. There is no misery on earth so painful or so impossible to get away from as a tortured conscience. Money can buy lots of things, but it can never buy happiness, never buy a clear conscience, never can buy that gloriously independent and free feeling that comes from one's own inner satisfaction.

> "And this above all, to thine own self be true,
> "And it must follow as the night the day
> "Thou can'st not then be false to any man."

ADVANTAGES OF TRUTH AND VERACITY.

If you never tell a lie you cannot be dishonest, for the first time you steal an apple or a penny or fail to return what you know belongs to some one else you tell a lie to your own soul and you act a lie by keeping the thing "sneaked," even though nobody knows about it but yourself and one other. There is always one other knows besides yourself —God knows and you know. Gladstone, when a boy, once took a thrashing from two older and bigger boys because he would not go to a neighbor and tell him a false story which the bigger boys told him to tell. He afterwards found out that if he had told that false story he would have received two whippings—one from the neighbor and one from his father when he found it out. It always pays to tell the truth.

HOW TO CHOOSE VOCATION AND LOCATION.

One of the most important things for a young man about to start in life is his choice of a trade or a profession or a line of work that he intends to make distinctly his own. The thousands of wrecks and failures in life are mostly, if not altogether, due to neglect upon this matter in youth. They simply drifted along, taking up whatever presented itself, and consequently soon found themselves in a business that they were not fitted for and disaster followed as a matter of course.

Every one is best fitted for some special sphere in life. Early inclination or aptitude is usually the best guide, and that parents should look for in their children and cultivate. Above all they should not go contrary to the apparent wishes of the child in order to have the child take up some pet vocation which the parents have set their hearts upon his following. Nature points the way in almost all cases, perhaps in all cases if we give heed to her still, small voice.

The same thing may be said regarding location. One thrives best where he is best pleased. If the location is distasteful it is usually better to seek one more in accordance with one's natural preference.

EVIL EFFECTS OF INTEMPERANCE AND PROFANITY.

Fun and hilarity are as natural as life   And it is right and proper to seek and enjoy them. But no one puts a greater stumbling block in his path than he who begins to form a habit of swearing or of drinking liquors. To see a drunkard or to hear a profane man for the first time is enough to fill any one with disgust. What sense then is there in any boy or young man beginning to do the things that after awhile will cause those who see them to feel disgust for them ? And worse yet, it is not long before you begin to feel disgust for yourself, and you can't get away from your own company.

Swearing don't help anything. It neither makes "one hair white nor black." It weakens every expression to which it is added. It is simply and purely a habit caught by contagion, like small-pox, and cultivated by practice till it deforms the person habituated to it and injures his chances in every career in life from the humblest to the highest. Do not begin to swear, or if you have already begun, quit. That shows sense and ability. It is only very weak persons who can t or won't quit. So, too, with drinking and all other forms of intemperance. Young man, do not take the first step to intemperance in speech, or deed, or thought. Or if you have already done so, stop now—now, when the call comes to you. Now is *always the best time.*

TOBACCO HABIT.

Do you know of anything more filthy and more useless than the chewing and the smoking of tobacco? Just think of making chimneys of your mouths and spitting smoke into other people's faces. Or to make a sewer of your mouth and chew and spit the vile brown juice from the wads made of the leaf of the weed, that no animal will eat, and known as the tobacco plant. Worse yet, when you know of the nasty way it is soaked and prepared and packed into, not over clean boxes, and handled by scores of dirty hands before it enters your mouth. It is a prolific source of dyspepsia. Smoking especially produces all kinds of nervous disorders, is one of the large causes of insanity and of kidney disease as well as of rheumatism and neuralgia. The nicotine contained in the poisonous weed is dangerous to health even when taken in minute quantities. The use of tobacco is one of the chief links that still bind the race to its ancestry of barbarism. It will never stand the advance of civilization. Let it severely alone.

INDUSTRY AND ECONOMY THE HIGHWAY TO WEALTH AND FAME.

What is it you want? Not now, but in your sober moments, when you think it over. A good time now—a little indulgence now and poverty and discontent for the rest of your life, or a little self-denial now, and years of pleasure after?

As sure as fate it may be stated that the only highway to wealth and fame is economy coupled with industry. The world is full of examples of brilliant, bright boys, who became poor, wretched, ruined men, while their ungifted brothers or neighbors have won ease and comfort or fame and riches. How was it done? Simply by the practice of economy in youth or before they had won independence and all along persistent industry. There is no royal road to fame or wealth. It is a universal experience that the path to success means tireless industry and the cutting off of the little leaks in resources that swamps so many every year.

Read over and over again the suggestions we have given. Abide by them and you will succeed. Disregard them and you will be sure to sink, perhaps to find a life of degradation and poverty. A life is not accident. Things do not "happen." As a man soweth so shall he reap. And if he sows nothing he will reap only the whirlwind.

ADVICE TO CHILDREN AND YOUNG PEOPLE.

BY HARRIET BEECHER STOWE.

On Obedience and Gratitude to Parents.—"Children, obey your parents," used to be the injunction forced upon us in our childhood days, but which in these times is falling into disregard. Children, almost as soon as they reach a school age, begin to do things contrary to the wishes of their parents and, unfortunately, too many parents are negligent about teaching the young in early life the value of obedience. The child, incapable of perceiving that the motive of parental restraint is the child's future happiness and welfare, thinks it is the suffering victim of the parent's power.

But it must not be forgotten that from birth to death we are all subject to higher law, and almost all our evils and our suffering in life come through disobedience. This entire nation, almost, suffers from dyspepsia, because in early life they had failed to learn to obey the laws of health in their eating and drinking. Government is possible only by having laws and by obedience to those laws. All success in business is made possible only by having some in control and all the rest obedient to the instructions given. Armies win battles only by the absolute blind obedience of the soldier to his commander. In fact, the necessity for obedience is apparent in every avenue and condition of life.

Success Won Through Obedience.—How absolutely necessary it is, then, that the young should have it impressed upon their minds, early, that obedience to rightful authority is their first and most imperative duty. Their chances for success and happiness in life depend very largely upon how well this lesson has been learned. In order to know how to command you must first learn to obey. The only true and natural place to learn this lesson is in the home. By yielding strict obedience to their parents, who are rightly set in authority over them, children learn to obey the laws of God, of nature, of their country, of society, of business, and by so doing can win success and happiness.

Evil Consequences of Ingratitude.—On the other hand, when a child disobeys its parents and becomes ungrateful for what they have done for him, it is not uncommon for the parent to disinherit such a child. Who does not know of Mr. George M. Pullman, the founder of the Pullman Palace Car Company, and his disobedient sons? Had it not been for others these ungrateful sons would have received comparatively nothing of their father's great wealth. And this is only one instance among thousands where children lose fortunes as the result of disobedience.

No words of condemnation can be too strong to characterize the base ingratitude shown by some children. After the parents have reared them, sent them to school, cared for them in health and in sickness, they turn about, and, forgetting all they owe, so shamefully treat their parents as to hasten them to the grave in sorrow and grey hairs.

It is a lamentable fact that the world is full of ingrates. It seems only too true what one aged grief-stricken parent said: It seems to be the rule that the more parents do for and sacrifice for their children the less gratitude they receive for it. After a whole life of labor and sacrifice, their last days are made infinitely worse than the first days of struggle by the sad ingratitude of their children.

How Parents Teach Their Children to Lie—I wonder if parents ever stop to consider that if even only once they threaten a child with punishment and ask for a promise "not to do so again" they are teaching that child to lie. It may sound harsh yet if they will stop to think, they can hardly expect any other result.

The young are impressionable, and easily led into right ways and still easier into the wrong ways, and it is the most natural thing in the world for a child to deny the truth if thereby it thinks to escape punishment. Scolding and whipping are both relics of barbarism. You can lead your child infinitely farther and much easier by love than with a whip or with sharp words and clouded brow.

Take Your Child to Church—The greatest uplifting influence in civilized life is the church and cold and cheerless indeed is the churchless community. Even the one who does not go to church feels the effect of its influence and receives the benefits that come from its presence. Its good offices reach out in countless ways and directions embracing the community in an atmosphere of unselfishness and morality.

We must develop in our children a love of morality for its own sake rather than righteousness based upon fear of the consequences of immorality.

Mere laws cannot create morality; force does not create righteousness. These qualities come from within, from the soul and from the enlightened mind.

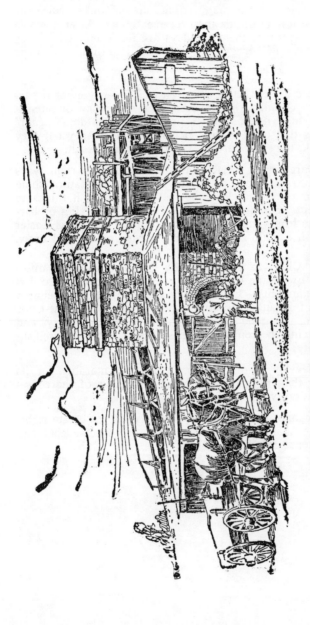

JOHN BLAKE'S HISTORIC OLD LIME KILN (North Carolina).

Lime is a safe, simple and effectual cure for Membranous Croup.

It was long a common belief in the old Pine Tree State that no child could die with Membranous Croup if treated with lime from John Blake's lime kiln, and from far and near people would send for this lime for that purpose. Later, it was found that lime from any other kiln was equally as good.

French Cure for Membranous Croup. Dr. J. R. DaCosta writes: "In our hospitals strong vinegar and salt has proved to be the most certain cure for membranous croup. I have cured the very worst cases with it, even patients over 50 years of age."

DIVISION FOUR.

HOME.

EY C. D. M. CAMPBELL.

This is one of the most common words which we all understand, perhaps, after our several fashions, but which none is able
precisely to define. It would seem to mean one thing to one man,
and something quite different to another, very much according to
the capacity, culture and disposition of each. Our ideas of home
are somewhat like our ideas of God. The Great Spirit of the savage
does certainly not much resemble the God of the enlightened Christian. Many of the attributes of these beings are just the opposites
of each other. But, behind the crude or imperfect notions of each
there might, perhaps, be discovered a Divine Reality, if one were
only wise and great enough to find it. So, though men differ
widely in their conceptions of what constitutes a home, there may
possibly be some common elements, apparent to the eye of a close
and exclusive analysis, in which all would agree, and which must
therefore constitute the real and only essentials of that substantial
thing which all men quickly recognize, but upon all the conditions
of which so few are entirely agreed.

ITS INDEFINABLE CHARM.

It would further seem that, among these essential elements of
home, and perhaps first among them, is a nameless if not wholly
indescribable charm. This is like the fragrance of an odoriferous
shrub or flower, which proclaims its neighborhood through miles of
distance, and is strongest in the silence and darkness of the night.
Something like this is the charm of home. The heart scents it
from afar, when the eye cannot behold it, and gloats on the ideal
picture of its beauties amidst the silence of solitude and the black-
ness of actual desolation. Hence, none have written more elo-
quently upon the charms of home than the homeless. The author
of "Home, sweet home," was a wanderer and an exile, and sang but
the passionate picture of his own sad and lonely heart. Rest,
peace, love, friendship, joy—these, and much more which we cannot name or characterize, are the constituents of that wonderful
charm which dwells in the word Home. These are the breath of

its fragrance and the odor of its thought. These, with the simple
utterance of the name, let into the heart, as through an open window, the light of beauty and the atmosphere of purity, and it is
these that render a home, whether real or fancied, "the dearest spot
on earth" to every man.

THE COMMON IDEAL.

The influence of this most wonderful and sacred of all institutions is, in its nature, purely centripetal, or attractive; it is the
gravitating force which restrains humanity from wide and lawless
wandering, and it operates in two directions; it pulls forward and
it drags backward; it incites to build, and it acts to restrain. Its
antitype is in the heart of every good man and woman. It is an
ideal picture, which all feel that they must somehow place upon the
canvas of their lives; an imaginative structure, which they must
build at the cost of all their earthly possessions, or life itself will be
destitute of meaning and of end. To this, they are naturally and
irresistibly drawn. This is the meaning of labor, of enterprise, of
thought, and of all the passionate attachments of the heart. The
visions of the youth, and the dreams of the maiden have this common interpretation. The apparently mysterious forces of sexual,
kindred and social attachments and aversions find here their clear
solution, and draw hence all their spring and energy. Love and
hate, friendship and dislike, coldness and indifference, the realities
of time, and even the visions of eternity, are inspired by this passionate longing for home. It is just because this longing is so seldom satisfied, this vision so rarely realized ; because the actual
experience of home has disappointed by its imperfectness and
pained by its discords; it is because of this that men and women,
despairing of their ideals in this world, have looked to realize them
in another and better, and so come to think that the disappoint-
ments of earth may be atoned for by the fruitions of heaven. It is
thus seen that the design of all theology, and even of all religion, is
the realization of this common desire for a perfect home, hell itself
being but the everlasting limbo to which the revengeful heart con-
signs the enemies and disturbers of its domestic peace.

ITS RESTRAINING INFLUENCES.

Imperfect, however, as is the home of earth, and far as it commonly falls short of realizing the ideal of youth and maturity, yet,
once built, according to man's best, it throws around him an indis-
soluble chain. To maintain it in being and add to its attractions,
becomes now the one purpose of his life and labor. For this, he
toils by day and watches by night. In the field, the shop, the office,
the laboratory, the library, the forum—everywhere—the worker
works for home. Allured to the paths of adventure, vice or crime,
he is held back by the tie of home. Driven to despair by want or

woe, and longing for the rest of the grave, the rash hand of the suicide in thought is paralyzed by the memories of home. Frantic with rage or bitter with revenge, the thought of direful consequences to those he loves curbs the wrath which might wreak itself in blood. If he is a good citizen—the conservator of those moral influences which hold society within the bounds of order and decorum—all this is due to the domestic stake he must venture for the gratification of an illegal avarice or illicit lust. In short, the factors of every enduring social state and the constituents of every permanent and advancing civilization, lie in the homes they embrace and of whose tender energies they are the crystallized expression. If there be virtue, honor, worth, purity and peace on earth, they were born in its homes and will perish with their extinction.

THE INTEGRITY OF HOME—THE SAFE-GUARD OF NATIONAL STABILITY.

The convulsions which occasionally shake society to its national centres and threaten the overthrow of all the institutions which Time has consecrated, issue from those apparently sudden and cyclic changes which periodically occur in the domestic temperature of the world. When at any period in the history of a nation, love becomes a jest, friendship a myth and honor a name; when the night of Despotism has settled down clear and cold and drear, extinguishing those fires of purity and trust which burned upon the hearth of home; then the wild ruffianism of the individual man breaks forth in anarchy and blood. As it was with France in '89, so will it be with every nationality on the earth; when the state, by its arbitrary social distinctions and unequal laws, invades and tramples upon the sacredness of home, it simply takes its own life; because the state is the product of its homes and has unnaturally destroyed those factors of which its dignity, grandeur and authority were the mere multiple. When the state becomes paternal in its government; when it undertakes to educate or to regulate, in any other interest than the conservation of the public peace, the children of its citizens, then it usurps the highest and dearest prerogative of the royalty of home, and it will, in time, snatch all the others; and then, indeed, it will have committed national suicide, for society will dissolve and go back to its original elements. The Spirit of Progress, so-called, who now stands embracing the pillars of the temple of our National Freedom, is the Blind Sampson, whose strength is coming fast, and who will soon bow himself to bury all in a common ruin.

THE FIRST CONDITIONS OF HOME.

Such, then, being the influence and effects of the home, it may be well, if possible, that we should form some distinct conception of its essential conditions.

The first of these is, obviously, the presence of one man and one woman, who have mutually chosen each other out of all the world, and who are held together by the same attraction of mutual and exclusive choice. This it is that makes true marriage; and those, and those only, who are thus wedded are true husbands and true wives. They may be of any faith, or of no faith. The ceremony which united them may be gorgeous and elaborate as that of Rome, or simple and natural as that of an untaught savage. The essential thing is, that they love and prefer each other to all the world. This being granted, they are the common centre of the circle of home. They make its earliest constituent, and its prime and essential condition. Without this, there may be much that is charming and bright, but there is no home. Indeed, whatever of brightness or of charm may be discerned in those broken circles to which this element is wanting, will be found, on a careful examination, to owe their presence to the sacred memory and still potent influence of this primal fact. If the children cling to the old roof-tree, under whose shelter sits the lonely and widowed husband or wife, it is because the vacant place was once so honorably and tenderly filled that the simple recollection of the lost has still the power to charm and bind. It is a power so enduring and sacred that death itself cannot quite cancel it. This, then—the presence of one man and one woman, joined together in a tender and sacred union of hearts—makes the earliest element of the real home.

CONSECRATED BY TIES OF PARENTAGE.

The next—and the immediate and proper consequence of this —is the presence of parents and children. When the loving wife ripens into maternity under the chaste and tender influence of her husband's embraces, she is not only fulfilling the ends of Nature and the law of God, but she is adding another and equally essential constituent to the home. Indeed she is helping, as in no other way so efficiently she can help, to build the home. Not all the domestic virtues combined can atone for the barrenness. This is the greatest of all misfortunes. Until her babe smiles in its mother's face and coos in its father's arms, their common being is incomplete. Strange and awful depths of tenderness are unsealed by the presence of the little one, whose waters could never else have purified and gladdened the hearts of the husband and wife. Holding this treasure in their arms, they taste a divine joy and unlearn the hardened selfishness of life. Their union is now first complete. They are not merely husband and wife, but the common parents of that bud of being which they see unfolding under their eyes; and this fact invests either with a new and unspeakable dearness to the other. It is no longer John and Jane, that each sees in the other, but the father and mother of my boy; and both feel that the mutual tenderness of wedded love bore no comparison to the mutual tenderness of wedded parentage.

And besides this, the birth of the little stranger has, in some new and mysterious way, made them akin to all humanity. The childhood of the world has crept into their bosoms and made its home there. They love all children for their own child's sake. Even the beggar's brat, which they were wont to pass with disgusted feelings and averted eyes, seems now to be invested with a new and inexplicable charm. Their eyes have been somehow unsealed, so that they can look through the dirt and rags down to the angel nature which they hide.

SACRED DUTY OF MOTHERHOOD.

It seems hardly conceivable that any wife could be willing to forego this divine joy of motherhood and this sacred duty of home-building, for the unnatural claims and doubtful pleasures of fashionable society; yet such wives we are assured there are, and not a few. In the larger towns and cities—the so-called centres of civilization—it is said that, with many society-ladies, motherhood is dreaded as a curse and prevented by crime. Undoubtedly, so far as they are concerned, the sin brings its own punishment, and the punishment is sufficiently severe. It makes no difference, that they are for the present unconscious and dreadless of that harvest of woe whose seeds their jeweled hands are sowing every day. It will come soon and fast enough. In broken health and blighted life—in loneliness and lovelessness—they will realize, at last, that they are reaping as they have sown. But the crime against society—the sin against government and race—the infidelity to marriage vows and obligations—the putting out of the light of a home—the blighting of human possibilities of greatness and worth—the destruction of a factor in the purity of society and the strength of a state, what personal suffering of the wretched criminal can atone for this? During an eternity of misery—could she suffer it—this sin would grow blacker by all the smoke of her torment, and greater with every groan of her anguish. The sufferings of the sinner cannot undo the sin; albeit, it is ordained, by the organic law of our being, that the sinner shall suffer. We see, however, still more distinctly, by the lurid light of such a crime against nature and society, how essential is that second condition of home, which we have named as the relation of parents and children.

HOME AN ABIDING PLACE.

Another of those essential constituents of home whose importance it would be difficult to exaggerate, is a dwelling-place. This, if possible, should be the inalienable possession of its occupants. Let it be altered, improved, amended, if they will and can, but never, save under the stress of urgent necessity, abandoned. The local attachments of our nature are strong and ineradicable. The popular proverb, "A rolling stone gathers no moss," is fairly applicable not alone to material possessions, but to those higher acquisitions which enrich the understanding and the heart. These are rubbed away and lost by the sharp attritions of local change, until one becomes a mere human boulder, the mechanical result of the circumstances which have swept, tossed, and washed him hither and thither, and left him lying helpless and supine, at the mercy of every elemental and impulsive force. The steady and unchanged homestead, on the other hand, is the soil in which the dwellers are infixed like the strong rocks, which laugh at the storms of life, and successfully resist all violent and injurious change.

HALLOWED BY ASSOCIATIONS.

In process of time, there are transferred to such a spot and made a part of it, innumerable associations, joyful or sad, but all alike tender and endearing. The graves of forefathers and mothers, the home-coming of brides, the departure of sons and daughters, the birth and death of children—all have left their traces on house and furniture and soil. These dumb, material things are eloquent of all the interests and emotions of the home circle. They bind its members to the spot, or force them, if they wander,

> "To drag, with every step, a lengthening chain."

Years afterward, indeed, when the family is extinct or scattered; when the fences are fallen down, the hearth-stone cold and the house a battered ruin; the footstep of a lonely stranger, treading there, is repelled by unseen forces, and something says,

> "As plain as whisper in the ear,
> The place is haunted."

Haunted, indeed and forever, it is, by the undying ghosts of the passionate hearts that once dwelt and revelled there.

So strong, so enduring, so imperishable is the influence of a dwelling place. No doubt, some cannot have it. It is out of their power to purchase and own their own dwellings. The necessity of their pecuniary circumstances or local surroundings forces them to rent and occupy, on such terms as they may, the hired tenements of others. This is especially true of the working classes in the cities. But even they may shun, as much as possible, removals from house to house. They may select a modest dwelling, at a price so distantly removed from the outer margin of their means as to promise permanence of occupancy if they so choose, and stay there ; and this will prove, in time, a tolerable substitute for ownership. Gradually, the place will grow warm and dear to them. Should their pecuniary circumstances solidly improve, then, instead of seeking another and more eligible situation, let them take a long lease of the one they now occupy, and proceed to renovate it in accordance with their better tastes and larger abilities. This will give them that fixedness of abode which is essential to home, and which no money expended elsewhere can purchase.

THE SPURIOUS HOME.

But a worse practice than that of frequent removals seems to be steadily gaining ground in the towns and cities; and that is, the custom of family-boarding. This, it is urged, is both convenient and cheap. The wife has more leisure for society, and the husband more time and money for business and pleasure. Neither is worried or hindered by the annoyances of housekeeping. All this may be true; though we doubt about the economy, from what seems to us the sufficiently significant fact, that poor families cannot afford to board. They make a home for themselves because they must. It would seem, then, that families board not because they cannot afford to keep house, but because they cannot afford to do so in a certain style which they deem essential to their social standing. If they could go to a grand and splendidly appointed house, they would all go to morrow, and we should hear no more of the conveniences of boarding. Then, it is to this false and tyrannical god of Social Appearances that they sacrifice their comfort, their privacy and their home; for in boarding they can have none of these. They cannot choose their own table, their own hours, their own company, or their own entrances and exits. They must go in and out, up and down, at the beck and call of others. Their children must be deprived of their natural liberty, of all wholesome discipline, and exposed to the baneful influence and injurious caprices of strangers. Above all, they must be homeless; for a boarding-house is not, and cannot be made a home for any one—not even for its keepers. And to compensate for all this they have two priceless privileges: The luxury of being considered respectable, and the liberty of grumbling; and it must be confessed that they exercise the last so constantly that, one would think, it must be inexpressibly dear to them. If its exercise, however, can compensate them for the ruin of two homes —their own and that of the family with whom they board—we must say, that they richly deserve that curse of homelessness which they suffer and inflict. However, should they be forced by kind adversity to abandon the boarding-house, though for the poorest tenement in all their knowledge, they will learn at last, with grateful and happy hearts, how much truth lives in the immortal line,

"Be it ever so humble, there's no place like home."

MORAL ASPECTS OF HOME.

No consideration of what is involved in the subject of home would be complete without some allusion to its moral aspects, and the mutual relations of those who constitute the household. Home is something more than the mere dwelling place, set apart for the physical comfort and convenience of its inmates, and without the presence of its higher attributes, and the realization of its moral duties and responsibilities, it is incomplete, if it be not the mere empty semblance of what the home should be. The complete home embraces within it limits a perfect system of social government, and it is in these integers of the aggregate community that there is to be found the highest guarantee of the stability of the whole social fabric of the state. It is not only the temple of domestic virtue, but it is the school in which men and women are qualified for their ul-terior duties of citizenship. Here in youth are learned the princi-ples of obedience to constituted authority, which in manhood are carried into the wider sphere of social duties. Here the edifice of character is founded; the moral stature trained to grow apace with physical and intellectual development, and the impress given which stamps its seal of expanding influence upon the future life, and its ever broadening associations.

Domestic Discipline—Nothing is more absolutely essen-tial both to the future well-being of children and to the proper har-mony of the household than that the youth should be thoroughly trained in the habits of obedience, and taught to honor and respect the parental authority. Filial respect is the surest foundation of an upright character, and it is the chief guarantee of the parents for the realization of the rewards to which they look forward for the care and labor expended upon the infancy and youth of children. Yet in no respect are parents as a rule more careless than in this. The true foundation of filial obedience is affection, which makes the duty a pleasure, and renders its performance doubly grateful to both parent and child. In order to insure the proper cultivation of this trait, the habit should be carefully inculcated from the earliest dawn of intelligence, until it becomes by custom a part of the nature of the child and is crystallized into character in the development of youth. Too commonly carelessness and indifference on the part of parents allow the child to drift without guidance in this respect, until they find themselves confronted with a hardened will set up in opposition to the demands of duty. True, the parental authority may then be asserted; obedience may still be enforced; but then a charm in the household is broken which can never be restored, a chord of har-mony severed whose music will never again vibrate in the heart of parent or child, and one of the sweetest of domestic pleasures will have been banished from the family hearth. That obedience of children which is founded from earliest infancy on love and respect, will blossom perennially in the hearts of both parents and children, and shed enduring fragrance upon every relation of life.

The Sense of Honor—It may be assumed that all parents, in discharging the solemn responsibility of forming the character of those whom they have brought into being, and whom they are called upon to equip physically, mentally and morally for the vicis-situdes of life, will take care that the character of the youth is founded in honesty, industry, sobriety, integrity, fidelity, economy, perseverance and self-reliant determination, which are the weapons in the armory of character by which success is to be wrested from all conditions. But too little attention is often paid to the true ground upon which these qualifications should be based. Youth should be taught in the lessons of the domestic hearth, both by precept and example, that it is not only necessary and desirable that honesty, integrity and industry are to be cultivated because they are essential to material success, but in a better and higher sense, because they bring even greater rewards in the moral duty of performance, and the consciousness of its upright discharge which is the true measure of self-respect. Character which is to be a blessing to its possessor and to all its associations, should be early grounded in what Burke describes as that "Chastity of honor which feels a stain like a wound." This is the highest safeguard of moral uprightness, and the surest shield against the temptations of life.

Sympathy—There ought to be few higher pleasures in life than the companionship of our children, whether it be in the prattling innocence of childhood, the buoyant exuberance of expanding youth, or the glowing anticipations of approaching maturity. The parent who can find no congenial companionship in his child; who cannot enter into its feelings, pleasures and aspirations with ready sympathy, may depend that he lacks something which is essential to his best realization of domestic happiness. Too often this is the result of the unhealthy habit of exclusive devotion to the absorbing cares of business, which robs so many of our people of the full enjoyments of the best rewards of life. Companionship, even *camaraderie* of parents and children is a mutual benefit as well as a mutual pleasure. It is a healthy and wholesome relaxation to the parent; it brings mental improvement and moral dignity to the youth, and it is the easiest road to the establishment of that perfect confidence, which should always characterize their mutual relations, and is essential to their mutual welfare.

Influence of Example—Among the influences which surround the home, none is more powerful in moulding the character of children and so impressing every aspect of the domestic relations, than the force of example in the various duties of life by the parent. How can parents expect or hope that their children will grow up in cleanliness of mind, manners and morals, no matter how assiduously the principles of rectitude are taught, who dishonor by their own practices the precepts they seek to impress upon the young? The power of example is stronger than the force of preaching. The very confidence and respect which children have by intuition for parents, adds redoubled force to the strength of pernicious example. You may teach a child that a habit is pernicious, but if you do not apply that rule to your own conduct, he will follow your example, and regard your advice as an abstract theory which it is not necessary to practice. If you desire your son to grow up to honorable manhood, be punctiliously honorable with him, even in the smallest things and from earliest childhood; see that your language and habits are cleansed from every taint from which you would guard his innocence; see that your passions are kept under control, and that your own dignity and self-respect are always maintained, and you will find not only the pleasure which you seek in the development of his character, but an added reward in the improvement of your own.

Home and Health—The laws of health make an imperative demand for ample seasons of recreation and relaxation from the continuous strain of the labors of existence and the cares of business. In no other place can pleasure and relaxation be found of as elevating and healthful a nature as among the pure and wholesome influences of home, in the loving society of wife and children. And yet to how great an extent are they neglected in the high-pressure rate of modern American life, depriving both the heads of families and their dependents of their best and most pleasurable associations, of their purest enjoyments, and of the best stimulus for renewed encounter with the cares of life. Even where those salutary influences are not neglected for doubtful if not injurious pleasures, it is too much the custom to bring the shop or the counting-house into the home. There is a lesson which might be learned with advantage by thousands of business men in the following extract from an article on this subject, in the *Golden Key*, by Mr. I. Harley Brock:

"If there be a fault to be found with the progressive, vigorous, energetic mode of life which is distinctively American, the characteristic of the healthy vitality of our people and their institutions, it is the tendency, too often developed, to allow the mind to become wholly engrossed in the care of business to the neglect of that large fund of resources for the higher enjoyment of domestic and social life, which every man with a sound mind in a healthy body inherently possesses. And this, when it does occur, invariably encroaches upon that period of life in which the capacity for rational enjoyment and wholesome pleasures is in its most vigorous stage. It is the too common mistake of the man of business to put off for the future day, when he shall have reached the affluence at which he aims, the exercise of that faculty of enjoyment which he robs of its present gratification with a promise to pay in the indefinite future, in order that he may redouble his attention to business pursuits. This is doubly a mistake, in that the future may never be reached; and if it be, then may be found that the time has gone by; that the capacity has perished in its neglect; that it is impossible to rekindle the fires of youth in the ashes of old age, and that when once resolved to devote the remnant of life to the pursuit of pleasure fairly won by arduous toil, there remains only the desire without the realization—able to 'clip Elysium, but to lack its joy.' He who keeps life well balanced, neither evading its duties nor refusing its passing rewards, will find in the end that he has made as satisfactory progress in worldly prosperity, and has lived a better and brighter life."

EDUCATION OF CHILDREN.

Among the chief of the duties and responsibilities of the heads of the Home, that which embraces the education of children is paramount in importance, and ought to be the subject of earnest and anxious forethought, and of unremitting and watchful care. The object of all parents ought to be, and is, except where unnatural and abnormal conditions exist, to bend the utmost energies and to strain every available resource to so equip the youth or maiden for their future life, as to best insure their happiness and prosperity. To this end, therefore, it is primarily of importance that youth should be endowed with a sound mind in a sound body—*mens sana in corpore sano;* and this embraces as well the health of the morals, for all experience goes to show that there can never be perfect or lasting physical and intellectual vigor without moral health. These three graces of manhood and womanhood go hand in hand through life; whenever one is absent, the others are certain to languish and decay. It is unfortunately the great defect of American domestic education that the moral side of life is not regarded, as it ought to be, as strictly essential to and belonging to the duty of physical and mental education. Perhaps no people in the world are so lavishly liberal in their treatment of the youth as are the people of America. The great masses of our citizens, having to carve their own fortunes out of their capital of industry and energy, find always the gratification of a laudable ambition which had been denied to themselves, in the effort to improve the social, intellectual and material fortunes of their children. The clerk or mechanic, forced by the hard exigencies of his early circumstances to forego many of the graces, refinements and luxuries of life, now that thrift and energy have made him the master of ample competence, finds peculiar pride and pleasure in taking care that his children experience none of the privations which he so well knows how to appreciate. The mother who in the springtide of her own existence was compelled to self-denial, is prone to take a lavish satisfaction, in indulgence in dress and social pleasures to her daughters. In both cases the instinct is natural and laudable; but it also contains the element of the very greatest danger to which children so situated are exposed in their education. Such indulgence is too apt to lead to pride of person, of position, and of purse, which warp and pervert the noblest, highest and most generous instincts of manhood and womanhood, and expose those so educated in false kindness, to the ever present risk of being stranded upon the shoals of utter helplessness by the first unexpected tempest of adversity. If the father, while denying no wholesome luxury or refinement of life to his son, were also to ground him upon those solid virtues of self-denial which he in his youth practiced from necessity; and if the mother without casting any shade upon the sunny youth of her daughters, were to teach them for their pleasure what it had been her task to practice in youth, the homely but substantial accomplishments of housewifery, these sons and daughters would achieve happier lives for themselves, and would escape many a trap and pitfall which the whirligig of time, in its eccentric and uncertain course, may bring them into contact with. Every son of wealth should learn a trade or calling; every daughter of affluence should graduate as a housewife. To affect to sneer at wealth is both absurd and vulgar, for in general its enjoyment implies the possession of some of the most worthy virtues; but the young should be taught this lesson, without which their education will never fit them for the highest and best achievements of life, viz.: that moral worth, not material wealth, makes up the highest dignity of manhood and womanhood; that well-earned self-respect is the highest reward any man can compass; that whoever possesses these, whether mechanic or millionaire, meet upon a common plane, and that upon the highest and best level of existence that human life can achieve.

Good Manners—While care is taken in the education of the young, that the development of physical perfection is accompanied by the healthy progress of mind and morals, what are called "good manners" must not be lost sight of. To paraphrase the catechism these are "the outward and visible sign of an inward and spiritual grace." They constitute the manifest expression of mental and moral health—not the expression of profession, but the spontaneous effusion of a well-constituted character. They are the blossoms which bloom upon the tree of worth and goodness, instinct with the fragrance of every virtue from which they seek the springs of existence. Good manners do not mean the mechanical observance of social formalities, the cold and unsympathetic routine of propriety. Courtesy of speech and manner, even if it be only following the adjunct to "assume a virtue if you have it not," is always pleasing and agreeable; but that is as "the tinkling cymbal," when compared with the grateful music which is awakened in the chords of a good heart by the impulses of an upright mind. Good manners, so considered, are the stamp which attests the unalloyed gold of a sweet and harmonious disposition, and no base or spurious counterfeit, however perfect the imitation or however bright and plausible the resemblance, can ever seek to rival its perfection. It should be the constant care of parents to teach the young that the courtesies of life are something real, and not a mere hollow form; and in training them in their conventional modes of expression, to gift the youth with those graces of character which shine out in good manners—deference and obedience to elders and superiors, respectful homage to the aged, chivalrous protection for the weak and feeble, sympathy with the unfortunate and even with the erring, and pleasure in adding to the happiness of others. These constitute true politeness, and their exercise is not only a principal charm of life for their possessor and those on whom they are reflected, but they are also a powerful influence in the promotion of the material welfare.

Care of the Person—When it was written that "cleanliness is next to godliness,"—whether it was meant to imply mere bodily cleanliness, or as well purity of the mind, the manners and the morals—there was a good deal more philosophy conveyed in the proverb than is expressed. The bath of the Mohammedan is a part of his religion, and strict cleanliness was one of the most rigid injunctions of the Mosaic law. It would be an inestimable boon to the physical welfare of modern Christian countries if this virtue of the Eastern infidels could be but made a part of the ordinary religious obligation. Scrupulous cleanliness of the person is something that one not only owes to himself and to his neighbors, but it is, as well, one of the most substantial comforts and grateful luxuries at our command, while the return in physical benefit which it confers ought to be in itself a sufficient incitement to its systematic cultivation. It is greatly to be feared that this is the point of all others where physical education in America is lacking, and that while, in a sense, personal vanity compels the preservation of a presentable surface, the fair exterior which our average citizen of either sex presents is but the whiting of the sepulchre. "Shall I wash for a high neck dress or a low neck dress, mother?" is a current witticism which points at what we must fear is, to a large extent, a palpable truth. How many hundreds out of every thousand go from month to month, without any other purification than the hand-basin affords, and yet would be unanimously indignant if the whisper "unclean" were ever so gently to assail them? In how many thousands of houses do we find the piano, but not the bath-room? And yet people consider themselves refined and cleanly, and have no conception of the horror and disgust with which they would regard the revelations which a Turkish bath might make for them!

The care of the person ought to be made a very essential part of the education which belongs to Health and Home, and strict habits in this regard should be scrupulously cultivated. The bath to even the youngest child should be graduated into a habit and cultivated into a luxury. As children grow older they should be taught the most punctilious and exact habits for the care of the person, and with particular regard to the hair, the teeth, the nails, and the hands and feet; not on the ground of vanity, or even of health necessarily, but as a matter of self-respect. These habits of the body will be conveyed again to the apparel, for the youth or maiden who has been trained to fastidious cleanliness of the person will not be able to endure contact with soiled linen, unpolished boots, frayed gloves or an ill-conditioned or untidily kept hat. The care of the person has these claims to our regard: It is essential to personal comfort; it is inseparable from personal dignity and self-

respect; when cultivated, it is transformed from a duty into a
wholesome and grateful luxury; and it brings a more abundant
return in the store it adds to the blessings of health, than anything
else within our power to compass. And moreover, it is the one
luxury that is within the reach of all, and for neglect of which no
one can excuse himself to himself.

Companionships—In the modern system of education, it has
been found that in forming the mind and directing the intelligence
of the young and impressionable, there is no mode of teaching so
effective as that of object lessons. As a matter of fact, until the
character has fully matured and during the whole period of the
greatest susceptibility and impressibility, the whole life of youth is
a series of practical object lessons. Those which he encounters in
the Home, we must assume to be of the healthiest and most elevating tendency; but the prudent parent will look well and watchfully
to the external influences to which their children are subjected. The
most potent of these is that of companionship, and in this regard
too great care cannot be taken that the associations are clean and
wholesome. The solicitude of the parent, however, in this regard
must be governed by discretion and judicious supervision. Too
frequently it is the case, either through carelessness or unintentional
neglect, arising from absorption in the cares of business, that the
young are allowed to drift into unprofitable companionship, and
when this is perceived it is sought to remedy it by restraint. Almost inevitably this results in re-action and serves to intensify the
danger. The best and most effective way is to so thoroughly imbue
the young mind with the pride of probity, and the sense of honor,
that contact with anything vicious or immoral arouses a sense of
repugnance and antagonism which is a certain safeguard against
contamination; and youth should at the same time be led to the
understanding that that which is simply idle and frivolous, though
apparently harmless, is the bridge by which the positively vicious
and immoral is reached. This is essentially true of the influence of books. Indeed, it may be believed that the companionship
of books has a more direct, absorbing and positive influence than
that of the social surroundings; and this is eminently and emphati-
cally true of youths of studious or sensitive disposition. Too careful supervision cannot therefore be exercised over what the child is
allowed to read. The fecundity of the printing press in these days
has let loose upon society an overwhelming flood of idle, frivolous,
vicious, utterly unprofitable and to a large degree prurient and
immoral literature, if it can be dignified by the name, which is a
constant menace to the mental and moral health of the young. It
is a mistake, however, not to allow the mind of the youth a sufficient pabulum of wholesome literary recreation. Wholesale and
unreasonable condemnation of reading for pleasure is almost certain
to drive the young to dangerous indulgence in secret. Rather
choose for him a fair allowance of clean and wholesome books of

useful and practical knowledge, conveying profitable moral lessons, and at the same time improving his ideas upon composition and his faculty of language. Lead him to understand and realize that companionship with the dime-novel, or the vicious class of fiction, is degrading and disgraceful, and you will thus educate his taste up to a refinement in such matters which will be his surest safeguard against the evil companionship of objectionable books.

SELECTION OF OCCUPATION.

The selection of an occupation is something which more concerns the ulterior objects of the home education, than those things which strictly pertain to the cares, duties, trials and privileges of the home circle. Home is the school in which the youth has received his mental, physical and moral training, and from which he is about to graduate with the diploma of paternal approval, sealed by the devotion, love and hope of the mother whose tender solicitude watched by his cradle, and whose fondest prayers will accompany him into the future which he is to make for himself. The choice of an occupation is something which may be and should be left to the decision of him who is to put all his future at stake upon it. But his qualification to make that choice will have rested solely upon the formation of his mind, of his feelings, or of his inclinations or prejudices, which rest to a large extent, if not solely with the parental function. And in this duty of guiding the inclination or interest which every youth has as to his career, into channels which shall best promote his future welfare and happiness, there is one rule that should govern alike rich and poor, high and low, and that is, that the dignity of labor, of duty, of life with an object in it, is essential to the true happiness and well-being of every human being. The man without an occupation—be he ever so high or ever so humble, born to purple or to penury, nursed in the lap of luxury or in the hard cradle of poverty—is an anomaly in life, a waif upon the bosom of the sea of existence, helpless, hopeless, purposeless; doomed certainly to wreck, disaster and destruction, either mentally, morally, physically or financially. All experience proves that in one or other of these shapes the fate of his useless being will overtake him. Let the children of the poor be taught that in whatever sphere of labor they may elect to work out their lot, if they but bring to bear probity and perseverance, honesty and earnestness and the sense of duty, all the best prizes of life lay open to them. Let the children of the rich be taught to respect the dignity of labor and to comprehend the vicissitudes of fortune, and while qualifying themselves for a wholesome and useful life in that more favored sphere in which they have been born, acquire also some practical vocation which shall never in any emergency leave them quite without the resources of self-respecting independence.